WOMEN & WORLD RELIGIONS

Denise Lardner Carmody

WOMEN & WORLD RELIGIONS

Denise Lardner Carmody

WOMEN AND WORLD RELIGIONS

Copyright © 1979 by Abingdon

Library of Congress Cataloging in Publication Data

CARMODY, DENISE LARDNER, 1935–
 Women and world religions.
 Bibliography: p.
 Includes index.
 1. Women and religion. I. Title.
 BL458.C37   291.1'7834'12   79-102

ISBN 0-687-45954-0

Scripture quotations noted RSV are from the Revised Standard Version of the
Bible, copyrighted 1946, 1952 © 1971, 1973.

MANUFACTURED BY THE PARTHENON PRESS AT
NASHVILLE, TENNESSEE, UNITED STATES OF AMERICA

for MARIE & BRUCE LONGBOTTOM

PREFACE

This book has grown out of my experiences in teaching courses in the world religions and women's studies. It is an effort to provide an overview of women and religion suitable for undergraduate interests or the general lay reader. Anyone familiar with the immensity of the topic will appreciate how abbreviated the presentation has had to be, and how significant the word "overview" has in consequence become. I can only hope that the book provides some sense of the whole and encourages those with special interests to pursue them further. The bibliographies supplied for each chapter, which indicate my own most direct sources, might be helpful in this regard.

A good many colleagues and friends have helped me with information or encouragement, and I have here the pleasant task of thanking Sydney and Robert McAfee Brown, Robert Cohn, John Esposito, Paul Magelli, Judith Plaskow, Roslyn Pope, Harold Schilling, Eloise Snyder, and Dorothy Walters. In addition I would like to acknowledge financial aid from The Institute for the Arts and Humanistic Studies, and the Research Office of the College of the Liberal Arts of The Pennsylvania State University for round-the-world travel in 1976. I was also supported by the Office of Research and Sponsored Programs of Wichita State University, and enjoyed the help and hospitality of the Institute for Ecumenical and Cultural Research, Collegeville, Minnesota, during the summer of 1978.

Finally, I owe special thanks to my husband, John Carmody, for criticism and a lot of typing.

—Denise Lardner Carmody

CONTENTS

INTRODUCTION

Women's experience with the world religions is practically coextensive with human culture, so let us try at the outset to focus our work by considering: 1) a brief theory of religion; 2) religion and contemporary feminist consciousness; 3) a world-historical perspective; and 4) this book's emphasis and content.

A BRIEF THEORY OF RELIGION

Religion centers in Mystery—in human nature's condemnation to a life richer than its understanding. Historically, religion has revolved around such questions as What is life? What is death? Why do we exist? Why must we suffer? From archaic times passionate concern about these questions has generated myths, sacrificial cults, and moral codes. Even today, religion still asks what promotes human wholeness, what fosters honesty and love, how "God" contends with evil and death. Even today the old questions remain, for divine Mystery, unlike a problem, lies beyond us, escapes our human ken.

"Mystery," then, is an alternative to "God," deliberately chosen to prick awareness that we do not know, cannot understand, the heart of the religious matter. We do, however, *experience* this heart, for it is implied in all our significant thoughts and affections. For instance, we experience Mystery each time we catch our breaths at the glory of a sunset or the depth of another's pain. In other words, we experience that anything beautiful or important inevitably involves life's overall meaning. In this way, we learn that Mystery is the substance of our spiritual lives.

The religions—archaic and modern, Eastern and Western— all have tried to express, communicate, and harmonize with such Mystery. They all have attempted to name it—to catch it as Being, Nonbeing, Void, Fullness, Father, Mother, or Spirit. Yet also, they all have acknowledged that Mystery escapes these names—that it is more unlike than like our designations. As the whole, it is always the "more," the "greater than" any particular part or designation. The ultimate warrant or sustenance for faith, in fact, has always been the overwhelming experience of Mystery's more.

Theoretically, one can argue that all persons are apt for Mystery, because all persons desire to know and love unrestrictedly. That is, these twin drives are insatiable: knowing never exhausts the urge to know; loving only increases the capacity to love. Further, each act of knowing or loving takes us "beyond." Useful understanding, for instance, is not what I wish or imagine or guess, but what is so. Through it, I transcend myself and encounter reality that is objective. Similarly, to love is to transcend self and seek what is truly good and valuable. It takes one into morality: If I cherish this value (for example, friend, country, justice), what am I going to *do* about it?

In this way, each act of knowing or loving can enhance my growth, can stretch me beyond my present self. So grown or stretched, however, I become a person who contends with Mystery, because all self-transcendence heads toward the totality, the whole. The goal of my knowledge, one might say, is the "beatific vision" that Aquinas foresaw. Only by grasping the cause of my world, its Beginning and Beyond, will my quest for intellectual light come to term. Similarly, only by coming to a pure (creative and healing) Love, will the "restless heart" that Augustine found at the center of human motivation gain peace. Therefore, if one keeps raising questions, keeps pursuing the grounds of one's judgments, keeps waging the fight for purifying love—if one is human in this signal degree, one homes to religion. Religion, then, is self-transcendence *par excellence*. It is the undertow of knowledge and love that carries us out to oceanic wholeness, to God.

Although all persons are therefore apt for Mystery and religion, because their constitutive drives set them before "God," such aptness can rust or deaden. This makes for the dullness called secularism, for when Mystery is banished, monotony weighs heavy. Then fear, busyness, or self-centeredness cramp the drive to know and love. Horizons narrow. Many are caught in the bubble of this world or their "me." Traditionally, the religions have condemned such self-confinement and preached (if not practiced) self-transcendence. Traditionally, they have tried to lead one from selfishness to personhood, from death to life, from pettiness to love. This has been their perennial humanism.

RELIGION AND CONTEMPORARY FEMINIST CONSCIOUSNESS

If religion centers in Mystery, and Mystery transcends sex (Paul's "in Christ there is neither male nor female" is a representative traditional line), then religious experience should transcend sex. In other words, the basal line in religion should be whether the person is open or closed, willing or unwilling to participate in Mystery. Nothing sexual draws this line. The radical honesty and love for which Mystery calls circumvent chromosomal differences. Yet it is also true that all religious experience comes to persons who are sexed, and that sex colors its expressions. Naturally, experience and its expressions interweave. Further, most religious experience is mediated through one's tradition. That is, the cultural assumptions into which one is born set up the kinds of religious experiences one is likely to have. So while no major religion would deny that Mystery can touch one directly, how one interprets such a touch is usually circumscribed by what one's tradition teaches. The glow of joy, the death of a child, the value of love, the role of sex, the way to peace, the place of self-denial—these manifold entries to Mystery normally are shaped or interpreted through a received tradition. What such traditions have said about the sexes, therefore, has shaped a great deal of what men and women have made of their best experiences—of their transforming insights, loves, and encounters with Mystery. One theme of this book, in fact, is that the religions have frustrated women's access to equality under Mystery by larding their experiences with perceptions of social inferiority.

Contemporary feminists are acutely sensitive to social inferiority. Those feminists who are also religious (open to Mystery) are therefore haunted by a dilemma: Must I choose between my feminism and my religion? Many feminists do in fact feel that the religions are irredeemably sexist. For them the religious traditions are that much more inauthenticity that liberation must raze. On the other hand, some feminists feel that to cut themselves off from Mystery would be truncating. It is no "liberation," they argue, to become dead-ended, dehumanized, separated from the beauty and power of a divinity that shows itself as love that can create and heal. So while they acknowledge much sexism within the religions, these feminists refuse to equate religion with oppression.

That is my position. Beyond doubt, the major religions of the world have a dubious record with regard to women. Beyond doubt, they have often been inauthentic mediators of religious experience. The very light and love within us that generate these judgments, however, are Mystery-borne—that is, religious. But because on occasion they *have* made possible this light and love, this religion, the religions have not been wholly corrupting. Part of our task, therefore, will be to winnow the wheat of authentic religion (genuinely liberating, viable yet) from the religions' sexist chaff.

Still, the chaff will be very prominent. For example, Buddhist women could not head the religious community. Hinduism usually held women ineligible for salvation. Islam made a woman's witness only half that of a man. Christianity called woman the weaker vessel, the more blurred image of the Image. Jewish men blessed God for not having made them women. Yet authentic religion, by each of these traditions' central confessions, holds most blessed honesty and love, which are hardly sex-specified. Each of these traditions, therefore, is a mixed bag. It has oppressed women socially while liberating many of them mystically.

Thus the religions, because they enroll human beings, are complex. Authenticity and inauthenticity vie constantly for their souls. Indeed the two are dialectically related, for authenticity is not something one has or gets once and for all. Often it is just pulling away from inauthenticity. In fact, each time one pulls away, one sees the need for further withdrawal. So an authentic woman is one who keeps plugging away at self-transcendence in knowing and loving, despite her inevitable setbacks or selfishness. So authentic religion is a tradition willing to pull itself out of the pits.

A WORLD-HISTORICAL PERSPECTIVE

One resource available today for reforming the religions' treatment of women is our contemporary world-historical perspective. Our age is one of an unprecedented confluence of cultures. Women from all walks of life and nearly all cultures are communicating with one another. Gatherings during the International Women's Year; articles and books about Asian women, Indian women, women in Brazil; television and newspaper accounts—these all publish the similarities and differences in women's status around the globe. In the midst of the cultural differences, I would emphasize two similarities.

First, there is a constant, core humanity. Women's socialization everywhere has tended to make them feel inferior to men, but nowhere has it destroyed their core drives to know and love. Moreover, their common subordination has tended to restrict women's abilities to know and love in similar ways. For example, mothers (Jewish, Muslim, Chinese, Hindu, Irish-Catholic) have all tended to emotional manipulation. Because they have had little official, institutionalized status or power, they have all been severely tempted to make spouses or children feel guilty. By communicating with one another, they can own up to this common temptation to inauthenticity and perhaps push beyond it to untapped strengths. Bonded in sisterhood, at least a few women can say they will do their utmost not to counter their societies' economic and political exploitation by emotional machinations of their own. Nonprofit, simply because it is right, they will fight with weapons of light.

A second common factor, despite cultural differences, is the influence of religion. Religion has been central to world history. Even a hasty reading of the major cultures' stories makes this clear. Archaic religions rendered the divine-human interactions compactly, producing the vivid rituals and myths by which most peoples, prehistoric and historic alike, have lived. "Higher" religions, East and West, somewhat broke with such myth-making, generating moral codes rooted in human conscience. But from Tierra del Fuego to Moscow, the religions have delineated all societies' world-views. Indeed, even when individuals spurned religion, they were living in cultures carrying heavy religious overtones.

For women, religion's effects have been crucial. In fact, to this day, much in women's social- and self-images remains religiously derived. For example, whore/virgin, mother/witch are contradictions charged with religious history. Foot-binding and abortion are similarly charged. Objective religious studies, therefore, can help women see many causes of their current plight. That is a primary purpose of this book.

THIS BOOK'S EMPHASIS AND CONTENT

This book's emphasis is on women's roles in traditional religious societies. More specifically, we will look at the traditional religious symbols of women's holiness and evil. Women's roles have, on the whole, been subordinate. Usually, a woman has gained status by belonging to a man—by being the daughter of this father, the wife of this husband, the mother of that son. Indeed, in few cultures was a woman's consent even needed for either marriage or divorce. The religious traditions of West and East, in fact, agreed that a woman should never be independent, ought always be subject. Thus, traditional societies regularly took steps to insure women's subjection or nonindependence. For example, Hinduism denied women the sacred thread, the symbol of religious birth. Buddhist nuns, while freed from familial supervision, were expected to serve even the youngest monk. Christian wives were taught to be silent in church and obedient to their husbands, for their husbands were their "heads," as Christ is head of the Church. Purdah kept Muslim women veiled from the eyes of all but their own men, partly because Islam measured women's salvation in terms of their submission, not to Allah, but to their husbands.

Relatedly, East and West were a twain that met in regulating women's education. How better to insure inferiority, they agreed, than by prohibiting intellectual growth? So, Hindu women did not study the Vedas, Jewish women did not study Torah, Chinese women did not pursue the Confucian classics. The theory that women ought to learn only wifely skills was promulgated the world over. Given the confines of her freedom and education, it is little wonder that woman's role traditionally has been wife and mother, not priest, rabbi, guru, or sadhu ("holy person").

If one studies the psychology behind this social positioning, one is struck by the richness and ambiguity in the religions' symbolization of women's holiness and evil. Clearly, one of the most pregnant signs of women's subordinate status has been the tendency to view them as either much better, or much worse, than men, for this implies that only men have normal, mid-range humanity. So women have been elevated as goddesses, virgins, mothers, symbols of purity, mercy, love. Likewise, they have been denounced as whores, witches, seducers, symbols of treachery, malice, lust. What they have not been, historically, is equal sharers of humanity whose social and religious offices have been determined principally by their talents.

Further, the balance of the religious symbolizations of women has fallen on the side of evil. There has been the pervasive myth of the devouring womb, cropping up in ancient tales, testimonies at witches' trials, and Freudian analysis. There has been the horrid Kali, Hinduism's female of blood and destruction, who wears a necklace of skulls. Buddhism has had the daughters of Mara (Satan) trying to seduce the Enlightened One from realization and promulgating the holy middle way.

Islam has populated the Fire with females, for they are by nature ungrateful "crooked ribs." Judaism and Christianity, finally, have offered their flocks Lilith, who dines on small children, and Eve, the source of humanity's curse. Consequently, our historical expositions often will be rather grim, amounting to an audit of debited accounts that the future must foreclose. However, as a small contribution toward this foreclosure, and a concretion of my conviction that genuine, Mystery-intending religion is liberating, we will conclude with some rather positive reflections on the good uses to which women's religious history might be put in the future.

BIBLIOGRAPHY

Bleeker, C. Jouco, and Widengren, Geo, eds. *Historia Religionum.* Leiden: E.J. Brill, 1969, 1971.

Bullough, Vern L. *The Subordinate Sex.* Baltimore: Penguin Books, 1974.

Daly, Mary. *Beyond God the Father.* Boston: Beacon Press, 1973.

Driver, Anne B. "Religion," *Signs* (Winter 1976) pp. 434-42.

Eliade, Mircea. *The Sacred and the Profane.* New York: Harcourt, Brace & World, 1959.

Gross, Rita M., ed. *Beyond Androcentrism.* Missoula: Scholars Press, 1977.

Lonergan, Bernard. *Method in Theology.* New York: Herder and Herder, 1972.

Otto, Rudolf. *The Idea of the Holy.* New York: Oxford University Press, 1958.

Streng, Frederick J. *Understanding Religious Man.* Belmont, Cal.: Dickenson Publishing Company, 1969.

Voegelin, Eric. *Order and History.* Baton Rouge: Louisiana State University Press, 1956-1974.

Wach, Joachim. *The Comparative Study of Religions.* New York: Columbia University Press, 1961.

Zaehner, R. C., ed. *The Concise Encyclopedia of Living Faiths.* Boston: Beacon Press, 1967.

ARCHAIC RELIGION

Archaic religion occurs in small-scale societies not shaped by the differentiation of science from myth. That is, archaic peoples tend to explain their reality in terms of stories originating from an imaginative, rather than a theoretic or scientific, penetration of reality. For example, they attribute natural occurrences such as rain or drought to divine powers, who are often seen as reacting to human goodness or evil. Such a world-view differs from our contemporary perspective, because it lacks the judiciously controlled thinking developed by modern science. For instance, archaic peoples do not clearly separate the sacred and the profane. For them all reality is potentially sacred—apt to carry religious Mystery and power. So, both the lightning and the tree it strikes may manifest the sacred, with the result that "reality" is tightly one, little differentiated into contrasting realms of natural/supernatural, common sense/theoretic, emotional/rational, and the like.

The religion of American Indians, Eskimos, African Pygmies, or Australian aborigines, then, remains "prior" to the introduction of scientific reason, still representative of a time when cultures stressed human beings' oneness with the cosmic powers. Historically, this cultural stress has been humanity's normal one, so in investigating the archaic view of women, we are dealing with attitudes that have shaped the vast majority of our forebears. Our investigation will have three steps. First, we will sketch the main features of the archaic religious mind. Then, we will look at some examples of women's roles and images in archaic societies. Third, we will try to summarize what these images and roles say about archaic women's religion, in the light of the archaic religious mind.

THE ARCHAIC RELIGIOUS MIND

Since archaic societies span from the oldest human ages to the present, the archaic religious mind has a time-frame of perhaps three and one-half million years. Further, since these societies, both prehistoric and contemporary, are basically nonliterate, the mind that we are probing has left few written records. The oldest human mentality, in other words, was oral and artistic, not scriptural. However, artifacts bearing religious symbolism that indicates a level of cultural development recognizably human seem to accompany all archaeological findings. It appears that as soon as human beings evolve to the point of being able to reflect on their condition, they begin to seek meaning, to probe Mystery. This indicates that religion is as old as humanity itself.

Now, it is dangerous to abstract from disparate archaic cultures anything like a regular or typical "mind." North America alone, prior to the coming of Europeans, had up to two thousand separate culture groups, many of them with mutually unintelligible languages. Still, among these tribes, and between them and other archaic groups, there do seem to be some important similarities, from which scholars can tender a few general hypotheses about early human culture. For our purposes, four characteristics are especially illuminating. Because of the compactness of the archaic world-view, they amount to four foci of archaic religion: the sacred, fertility, mytho-ritualism, and the shaman.

The *sacred,* for archaic peoples, is what is truly real. It is the basis of vitality and order. Thus, a first religious problem or charge for archaic peoples is the fact that human beings can live in passionate union with the sacred, and so feel whole, or can be distracted from the sacred, and so feel divided or "fallen." This is a primary archaic equation: to live in harmonious union with the sacred, the vital power coursing through the sky, earth, and sea, is to experience peace, joy, and fulfillment; to be unsynchronized with the sacred, through ignorance or bad will, is to court disaster. Moreoever, the sacred is no delimited, "Sunday only" sort of reality. It is constant and all-pervasive. Consequently, archaic peoples feel that each day brings them evidence of their union with ultimacy, sacrality, or their rupture from it. A successful hunt, rain for the crops, good health, tribal peace—these prove a people are in harmony with the real, the holy. On the other hand, no game, drought, disease, and bickering or war suggest that individually or collectively they are dangerously out of joint and need to have their balance restored. In this way, the sacred, the realm of power and the truly real, is both concrete and mysterious. Why or how it acts as it does may be hidden; that it does act is as obvious as any day's joy or sorrow.

Further, the archaic mind concretizes the sacred by making everything a candidate for its operations. Earth and sky, stones and animals, work and sex, birth and death—all creation is its realm. Indeed, archaic humanity seems to feel the pulse of the sacred in anything awesome, beautiful, or fraught with power. The sacred, then, is the context and inmost import of all human work. Hunting, planting, weaving, metalworking—all archaic occupations feel its touch. Among some hunting groups, for instance, men whose wives are pregnant will hunt only if in dire need. They believe that life is holy and somehow one, whether it quickens human, animal, or plant. Since pregnancy is a sacred event, it is inappropriate for those involved with it to kill beyond what they need for survival. Similarly, many gathering peoples ask pardon of plants before harvesting them. One Indian prayer, in fact, explains to the plant that its bark will become a baby's clothing. Besides its more dramatic revelations in vision quests, ecstatic trances, and natural phenomena like earthquake, volcanic eruption, or eclipse, the sacred tends to weave through all archaic culture.

Finally, and for our purposes significantly, archaic peoples regularly represent the sacred as androgyne—at once both male and female. In fact, androgyny is a universal archaic formula for wholeness, strength, and autonomy. It seems that sacrality or divinity must be androgyne if it is to carry its overtones of ultimate power and supreme being. However, this formula does not eliminate separate gender, because sexual differentiation is considered to derive from such primal androgyny. It is conceptually secondary, or later in order. Therefore a Sky-Father god and an Earth-Mother goddess may both be androgyne—equally primally divine. Consequently we can speak of a typical archaic realization that femaleness and maleness are coeval, co-present in the originating Mystery which transcends them both.

Fertility, a second focus of the archaic religious mind, vividly concretizes how the sacred penetrates the natural realm. To appreciate this, however, one must understand that, in archaic life, sheer survival is a primary occupation. Survival, in turn, entails an adequate supply of food and children. The first religious interests were therefore the first human ones: how to draw from the mysterious powers the wherewithal for the individual and the race to continue. Beyond what we might call practical measures—hunting, gathering, avoiding illness, begetting and protecting children—there is evidence that prehistoric peoples, like nonliterate peoples today, had recourse to religious survival-means. For instance, from Siberia to the Near East, figurines of pregnant women, paintings of men and women engaged in fertility dances, animal forms with prominent genitals, and the like, suggest magical ceremonies for both human and animal fertility. The famous paleolithic mural, the Sorcerer of Les Trois Frères, found in a French cave, probably depicts a "master of the animals." He has human feet but reindeer antlers, the ears of a stag, owl eyes, the paws of a bear, and the tail of a horse. Very prominent are his penis and testicles, and the entire personage seems clearly a product of ceremonial imagination designed to summarize powers of fertility and hunting.

Another aspect of archaic fertility is its concern for survival after death. There is evidence that more than a half million years ago, in the Dragon Bone Hill caves of China, near Peking, people were buried with hope for life after death. In other locations, they were buried in fetal postures, as if to suggest that the grave is a womb. This indicates that some of the earliest peoples tried to break death's stranglehold through intuitions that "something" may survive it. In their myths this something probably appeared as the part that travels in dreams, that can imagine realities other than the physical, that is like the smoke that fire releases from wood, or is part of a plant-like cycle of fallow and flowering. Such a "soul" could linger after death, giving ancestors a quasi-physical survival—something more than endurance in the memories of their offspring. It could also have brought archaic people to think of death as a passage to another life, where a subtler existence would be possible. Then, on return, one's life-force could animate another breathing creature, even another human being.

Fertility, then, is a matrix for the archaic concerns of life and death—life against death. Whether it led archaic peoples to conceive a single, overarching power (any "God") is still debated. It seems more likely that the most general archaic conception is of a universal bounty—a source of the natural and human life that keeps being replenished. Two apparent carriers of this providential power are the sky and the earth. The sky, vaulting over everything, seems in a position to observe and control. Perhaps because it houses the sun and the rain, the sky seems to have attracted the archaic mind's search for an ultimate principle dispensing vital energy from above. And the earth, as harvesting was connected with human birthing, seems to have assumed a maternal modality—to be the prime concretion of the Great Mother who is the source of all life. Thus, the cult of archaic peoples, their worship, often focused on generative powers. Among prehistoric groups, such worship probably associated the sky with masculine storminess and fertilizing rain, the earth with feminine gestation and cyclical fecundity.

Mytho-ritualism is archaic peoples' basic mode of expressing their meaning—their oneness with the sacred, with one another in community, within themselves as individuals. Myths are the mode of explaining what happened by telling its tale. "History," therefore, began in the mythic tendency of peoples to tell the tales of how they came to be where and what they were. Contemporary, "critical" history, of course, separates itself from myth by a rigorous control of its sources and arguments.

Nonetheless, it could not have developed without the prior capacity of human beings to hold in imaginative memory what had happened to them and what the events meant. "Ritual" refers to the conduct of ceremonies. In the archaic context, it connotes the actings-out, the dances and dramatic modes of participation, through which tribes indwell their mythic histories and realities. Together, myth and ritual fix the characteristic ways that archaic peoples have situated themselves in the world, interacted with the sacred, vitalized their community solidarity, and bedeviled scientific observers.

Remembering that there is no single archaic religious mind, but only many individual minds with shared characteristics, we may illustrate archaic mytho-ritualism with two creation accounts. Both evidence a conviction that the world has arisen by design and that human beings have been fashioned by deliberate divine action. Neither yields what modern Westerners would call a scientific theory of creation, but both bear shrewd insight into the human condition.

The Winnebago Indians picture creation as a process of pure divine thought. When the Father, the Earthmaker, came to consciousness, he cried because he did not know what to do. Noticing that his tears, which had fallen from heaven, had become waters, he realized that by wishing, he could make many other things become. So he wished light and earth, which became. Then he made a likeness of himself from earth. When it did not answer, he made it mind and soul, breathing into it so that it could respond. For the Winnebago, therefore, creation was willed; and human beings have a divine origin, likeness, and purpose: they have been made to speak with God.

The Central Eskimos of the Canadian Arctic have a female deity, Sedna, whose creative activity was more complex. In one version of their myth, she lives on the bottom of the sea, having been tossed from a boat by her father (he chopped off her fingers, by which she was clinging to the boat). Her fingers became the various sea animals—seals, whales, walruses—vital to Eskimo survival. In another version, Sedna and her children by a dog-husband were abandoned on an island by her father, who had caused her dog-husband's death. Sedna fashioned the soles of her boots into ships in which she sent off her children, some to become ancestors of Indians or spirits, some to become ancestors of white people. (None became ancestors of Eskimos, perhaps because, like most archaic peoples, Eskimos considered themselves the ordinary version of humanity and so were more intrigued by the exceptional humanity of whites, reds, or other foreigners.)

In the Sedna myths, creation occurs in several ways: biologically, volitionally, and "physically." Sedna gives birth, is the material source of the sea animals, makes ships from shoes, and, in still another version, wills a dead child back to life. Jumbled together, therefore, are Eskimos' awareness of female fertility, interest in the connection of sea animals with divine generativity, and sense that the life-power may be willful. (We pass over the rich psychoanalytic suggestion in Sedna's relations with her father, except to point out that Eskimos practiced female infanticide.)

Scholars have pointed out that creativity by the transformation of Sedna's fingers and boots may be linked to the roles of women in Eskimo society. There women create the waterproof clothing, tents, sleeping gear, boat covers, and so on, without which the tribe could not survive. Moreover, they make these vital necessities from animal skins—sea animal skins, in the case of tribes who live near water. Such work is shrouded in taboos, some of which amount to time restrictions as to when the women can work. The women thus do much of their creating in a frenzy, at breakneck speed, and perhaps seem to "work their fingers off." There may be a parallel, then, between female work that provides many of the tribe's necessary artifacts, and the divine work that provided the world's living artifacts. If so, one could explain the ritualized character of much female work, adducing menstrual taboos and seasonal ceremonies as further evidences that the Eskimo thought-world is lively with mythic parallels between sacral powers and human tasks. In other words, the divine creational work—fingers into animals, boots into ships—is the paradigm for human creation—animal skins into useful products. (In addition, Eskimo women's sacral work disputes the facile anthropological assumption that archaic women pattern with nature, while archaic men pattern with culture. More about this will follow.)

Because creation is the most fundamental mythic theme to which archaic ritual, in its core design to integrate human beings with the sacral cosmos, most frequently recurs, scholars have lavished much attention on the variety of archaic creation myths. They have found, for instance, that, besides what we have seen, there is creation by diving under the primordial sea to draw up the land, by animal sacrifice, through a cosmic egg, by sexual intercourse, by human dismemberment, and by masturbation. Relatedly, the rituals enacting these creation myths take many forms. Not only are individual activities such as sewing, smithing, planting, or building a home homologized ("done in the likeness of ") to the creation account, but in New Year festivals, the account itself is recited and reenacted, for each year the whole cosmos must be recreated for the next round in its cycle. In such festivals there is a psychological counterpart to the theme of the world's vanishing back into chaos and being drawn forth into order, for archaic peoples regularly make the New Year's celebration a time of licensed chaos (orgy) and then a reaffirmation of their stringent moral disciplines. So whether in explaining the origins of crafts, providing the context for birth and death, crowning rulers, or attempting serious healing, archaic peoples tend to try to reconstruct their reality by repeating the creation account.

Finally, we must mention what scholars call "rites of passage." These are the ceremonies of the life cycle—the rituals attending birth, puberty, marriage, and death. Each of these times presents a threshold to a new stage of development, which means a new stage of intimacy with the sacred. In tune with the divine archetypes, with what was done "at the beginning," one carries out obstetrics, the passover to adulthood, nuptials, and funerary rites. Among the most impressive of these rites are those for puberty. Rites for young men regularly stress the endurance of suffering. Rites for young women, whose accession to maturity is more dramatically marked, stress preparation for feminine tasks, as the particular society conceives of them. For both sexes, puberty passage is a time for instruction in sexuality, the nature of the tribal gods, and the discipline that mature responsibilities demand. Also, birth, marriage, and funerary rites are times when all tribal members can once again reintegrate themselves with the sacrality revealed to human beings through their temporality, their pilgrimage toward death.

Thus far, we have considered three foci of archaic religion: the sacred, fertilty, and mytho-ritualism. While we separate them for cognitive clarity, it must be repeated that they are integrally connected. For instance, the sacred, the Mystery that pervades all reality, is often concretized in archaic peoples' concern with fertility. In turn, fertility colors not only the archaic conception of sacrality, but the mytho-ritualism through which it is dramatized. The *shaman,* our final focus, is the religious functionary who most regularly expresses the archaic religious mind. In taking up the shaman's role, then, we are simply shifting to a more personified instance of the sacral-fertile-mytho-ritual complex.

The shaman, Mircea Eliade says, is a specialist in archaic techniques of ecstasy. And shamans of Siberia, where the term originated, and Central Asia gain their ecstatic powers by "conquering" death. The initiation motifs and ritual functionings of shamans in other areas—Southeast Asia, Indo-Europe, North and South America, China or Tibet—make the conquest of death less prominent. Paralleling this, the method of selecting a shaman varies from area to area. In some places the office is hereditary, while in others the selection process is more dramatic—the person is believed to be designated by solitary brooding, epileptic seizures, or strange natural occurrences (for instance, being struck by lightning). Finally, while many shamans are male, most cultures admit shamanesses, and in some, such as the archaic Japanese, women (often blind) have predominated.

In Siberian shamanism, which is often used as a prototype, once the candidate has been selected by elder shamans, he is taught their traditional lore and techniques. Next he is subjected to a critical initiatory ordeal. This amounts to an ecstatic, ritualized experience of suffering, death, and resurrection. The candidate may be dismembered, wrapped in icy sheets which he must dry with his "magical heat," have certain organs replaced or renewed (depending on the tribe's beliefs about what is the vital core of life—heart, liver, bone). What is constant in the ordeal is bodily sundering and death. The candidate dies, is taken to the realm of the gods, and is restored by divine agency, often reconstituted with new, magical organs. In this way, he becomes a mediator between heaven and earth.

After he has returned from the gods, the new shaman begins to function for the community. Healing, guiding the dead to the gods, and acting as a medium between the living and the dead tend to be his most important tasks. Such tasks reveal much about archaic beliefs. For instance, shamanic people clearly have a dualistic conception of the human person and the universe. That is, their universe divides into the human realm, where the shaman's body remains, and the heavenly realm, where his separable spirit travels. By ecstatic techniques (singing, dancing, ingesting tobacco or other narcotics), the shaman frees his spirit from his body and travels to the gods. This is his regular recourse when healing or caring for the spirits of the deceased—indeed, whenever his people need divine power or guidance. Thus, in times of sickness, crop or game loss, or danger of any kind, the shaman will sing, dance, invoke his helping spirits, mount his drum and "fly," or climb the cosmic tree to heaven for help.

The preceding depicts what might be called a shamanic prototype. We will examine the most relevant variations, those of Japanese shamanesses, later. We must note here, however, that shamanism may be extended to include such ecstatic phenomena as the vision quests of American Indians and the divinations of archaic Africans. Since the vision quest (seeking a personal revelation of one's guiding spirit) was a regular feature of the male puberty rite, it extended shamanism to the majority of male American Indians. Similarly, divinatory trances, to read the future or commune with the departed, gave many Africans, women included, an experience of ecstatic escape from their ordinary limits. Generally, then, shamanism suggests that ecstasy activates something that archaic peoples perennially have found both possible and desirable. For to go out of oneself, in order to deal with supernormal, paranormal, or even abnormal powers, is a way of extending one's world. It is a way of transcending oneself and, in many cases, of serving others. For the majority of archaic peoples the shaman has shown a way to the holy—to the really real, the Mystery, so fearsome and alluring.

WOMEN'S ROLES AND IMAGES IN ARCHAIC SOCIETIES

Having viewed some characteristics of the archaic religious mentality, we can now ask about the roles and images that it tends to set for women. First, while the archaic woman's lot is far from easy, the preponderance of evidence indicates that she is valued as one whose sacred fertility affects the tribe's survival, and whose economic role is vital. For example, in hunting and gathering groups, such as the African Pygmies, women both assist in the kill as beaters and furnish the vegetarian parts of the diet. Among some Native Americans, women farm and turn the game that the men have killed into food, clothing, and domestic implements. As shamans and diviners, many archaic women have high status and, generally, archaic people venerate all women's maternity.

One way to interpret the feminism of archaic religion is to stress the androgynous character of archaic sacredness, projected from the sexes' economic mutuality, and the archaic preoccupation with maternal fertility. Specifically, this invites discussion of the Great Goddess fertility religion. The scholarship in this area is still in its infancy, and we do not know what it will finally produce. What follows is merely a distillation of the hypotheses that currently seem most fruitful.

There is considerable evidence, first, that a female deity was worshiped during prehistoric (paleolithic, neolithic) and early historic times. The area of this worship spans from Spain to the farthest reaches of Russia. Second, while the Great Goddess was called by many names and revered by many cults, the similarities among her names and cults outweigh the differences. As a result, it makes good sense to speak of a single, semiunified Great Goddess religion. Statues of pregnant women, symbols believed associated with female fertility (snakes, certain trees), myths depicting the Goddess manifoldly, rituals centered on maternity—these are so omnipresent (in a vast circle perhaps centered on the Middle East) as to suggest powerfully a somewhat uniform religious culture, or at least cultural stratum, dominated by the Great Goddess.

Third, one hypothesis to explain the pervasiveness of this Great Goddess religion links it to archaic peoples' belief that reproduction is solely the "creation" of the female. Archaic peoples saw women waxing pregnant and giving birth. Female creativity, then, was quite public, manifest, obvious. The male role in reproduction, on the other hand, was less obvious, more hidden. Consequently, the great task of racial survival, of producing or expressing the sacral fertility necessary to defeat death for another generation, accrued to women. In other words, given the sacredness surrounding birth, it is quite reasonable that women were thought to share in a divine creativity, a great cosmic maternity. For, again, all humans tend to construct "divinity" by extrapolating from humanity. It makes good sense to hypothesize that the Great Goddess represented an archaic conclusion, arrived at from the human experience that early peoples found most mysterious, awesome, and crucial—the creation of new life.

Whatever one's hypothesis, there is an enormous amount of archaeological and mythological data collocated around the Great Goddess and awaiting explanation. There are world-creator goddesses in Sumer, Babylon, Egypt, Africa, Australia, and China. There are female divinities credited with having created specific cultural arts: India, Ireland, and Sumer, for instance, have goddesses who invented the alphabet, language, and writing. Other cultures trace agriculture and medicine back to kindly goddesses. The Sioux Indians attribute the origin of the buffalo to a sacred, beautiful, feminine divinity. Insofar as the foregoing extrapolation hypothesis has merit, we must conjecture that archaic women made signal contributions to their tribes' languages, farming, and healing. All these activities, in the archaic mind-set, were associated with the sacred. For them to be ascribed to *female* divinities, then, argues that women were their principal mediators.

More complex, perhaps, is the military power implied in the Amazon myths of Libya, Anatolia, Bulgaria, Greece, Armenia and Russia. Either archaic women did indeed fight alongside men, or their sexual power and female societies' authority raised a certain militancy in the early consciousness of women's potential. Lastly, perhaps the "ordinary" behavior of women, since they were valued in early societies, generated the widespread reverence for the Great Goddess' wisdom that we find. Pre-Christian Celts, for example, worshiped Cerridwen as the Goddess of Intelligence and Knowledge. The Greek Demeter and the Egyptian Isis were lawgivers—wise dispensers of good counsel and justice. Egypt also celebrated Maat, the Goddess of cosmic order, while Mesopotamia's Ishtar was the Prophetess, the Lady of Vision and Directress of the People.

Indeed, in eighth century BCE Nimrod, where Ishtar was worshiped, it seems that women served as judges. For just as it is logical that societies which stress the fertile sacredness of women might worship the Great Goddess, so it is logical that such worship might enhance women's social status. And, in fact, there is evidence that archaic cultures did indeed treat women more equitably than most later societies did. Specifically, the birth of a female was often a blessing; women had prestigious religious ceremonies; they could be scribes, healers, or counselors; the tribal memory accredited many cultural gifts (for example, the Australian men's ceremonies) to feminine discovery; women could participate in communal decision-making. For this reason, many scholars opine that Great Goddess cultures were more pacifist than warlike, more democratic than autocratic.

Finally, a word about one ritual associated with the Great Goddess religion, fiercely denounced by later, male-dominated religions (Judaism, Christianity, Islam): temple prostitution. The term itself, of course, is one given by the critics, who were castigating this elevation of female sexuality as harlotry and filth. (The vitriol in the attacks says as much about the critics' fears as it does about the "prostitutes' " actions.) From our distance, it seems that the Goddess cultures felt very strongly that sex and sexual intercourse were holy—hierophanies: revelations of the sacred, ways to union with the sacred. If this be the case, the sexual activities of the temple women, the Goddess' closest devotees, were acts of worship, not debauchery. (Both Hinduism and Buddhism developed Tantrism, where sexual intercourse was considered a religious vehicle, but Tantrism mainly served males' progress).

Moreover, the Goddess cultures appear devoid of the practice of stigmatizing some children as illegitimate. Since they were matrilineal societies (a natural outcome if women alone were believed responsible for offspring), a child's legitimacy rested with knowing its mother. All children, then, could be legitimate. Patriarchal cultures, on the contrary, had to be able to prove the paternity of each child, since their bloodlines, inheritance, and legitimacy were through the father. When the patriarchal, prophetic religions (Judaism, Christianity, Islam) met the Middle Eastern Goddess practices, powerful interests came into conflict. Masculine self-control, social authority, and theological construction (a masculine God) were all bound to see the Goddess temple worship as extremely threatening. Since the patriarchal religions won the battle, their scriptural and cultural authorities became "orthodoxy," and the female-oriented fertility religion became foul deviance. The resulting social subordination of women and circumscription of their sexual activity is a major theme of our later chapters, but here we must at least enter the slim warning that the Goddess devotees, far from being debauched, may simply have been expressing an experience of sacrality quite healthy and natural, because in their societies, *women's* sacrality was given its due.

From the scanty records of prehistoric and early historic archaic religious societies, then, we may conclude that women's roles and images centered on their maternal fertility, reflected a strong worship of a female divinity, assumed that they were strong cultural sources, and generally produced a cultural or political participation and respect that few later, supposedly higher, religious societies could match.

Moving forward in time, we come to other peoples whose archaic world-view is more open to research because they or their descendents are still living. Two such peoples are traditional Africans and Native Americans. While research into their feminine rituals, a major source for women's roles and images, has been scanty and is only now accelerating, it is clear that the women have ceremonies at least as detailed and valued as men's. A very positive instance occurs among the African Pygmies of the Congo, who view the menarche joyously, as a time for both personal and tribal celebration. For them the blood is a gift, an occasion for gratitude, a call to celebrate life. Pygmy women reflect this attitude in many ways. Indeed, young girls look forward to menstruation eagerly. When it comes, they go into seclusion to learn the lore of the tribe from their mothers and other female relatives. Then, having rejoined the tribe as young adults, they enjoy a time of partying, with activities that allow them, as new women come of age, to select their future husbands. The bearing of the young women strikingly projects their self-confidence, their pride. Finally, as the prolonged celebration testifies, the Pygmies, unlike many other religious peoples, share news of the menarche with no mention of pollution, shame, or fear.

The Africans of Sierra Leone also evidence a positive evaluation of women, for in their society, females have both self-esteem and social respect. Significantly, this is rooted in religion, for both women and men have religious societies that exert great control over their lives, especially during puberty rites. Sande, the women's society, is organized into local chapters. A girl is received into her mother's chapter (matrilineal social basis), but after marriage, she joins the chapter in her husband's village, where she has gone to reside (virilocal social basis). Normally, she will return to her natal village to deliver her children, often having as midwife the woman who helped initiate her into adulthood. By this linking of their chapters, the Sande women form a support network that provides social services and religious and civil influences far beyond individual village boundaries.

For instance, since women have a voice in marriage proposals, the Sande is a vehicle for consultations between male and female kin of both bride and groom. Thus, contrary to the view that archaic women are pawns passed from father to husband, Sande chapters allow women considerable self-determination, letting them move freely among parents, in-laws, males of both camps, and women of other villages. In fact, the Sande is a great source of tribal unification, for it moves women across even ethnic and language differences.

The *majo* or headwoman of each Sande, accordingly, has weighty responsibilities. She oversees the puberty rites, to guarantee their authenticity; she is a repository of gynecological advice and assistance; she dispenses a wide range of medicines for psychological and physiological ills. Indeed, a venerable majo is apt to travel widely, for she will be invited by neighboring Sande chapters to help with puberty rites and healings. On the basis of demonstrated competence, she will become a trans-chapter figure of no little influence politically and culturally. Her own local chapter will support her in her travels, too, because her reputation and influence redound to its honor.

The initiation rites by which a young woman enters the Sande and adulthood follow a traditional pattern of seclusion and instruction. The instruction deals particularly with the initiate's future tasks as a good wife and farmer. Since Sande women can expect to be co-wives (their society is polygamous), it is important that they develop deep sisterly ties, lest their husbands play them off one against another. Developing these ties is one purpose of clitoridectomy, the practice of excising the initiate's clitoris. This painful process is performed amid strong group support, for the other women console the initiate with food, songs, and dances. They help her to believe that her present suffering will ensure her future fertility and be a sign to her husband of her moral and social maturity. (Young men have their backs lacerated at puberty, as a similar passage to responsible adulthood.) Scholars also opine that clitoridectomy removes any "maleness," the clitoris being perceived as a penis-like organ, allowing the woman to fit cleanly into her female social status.

One can see that the Sande, with its multiple cultural functions, complicates or even confutes the anthropological notion that archaic women are solely allied with nature and archaic men with culture. In the Sande, women are taught from puberty through childbirth to exert strong cultural control over their natures. In fact, Sande women are forbidden to engage in promiscuous sex and must bear and nurture their children according to a definite code of hygiene. This is far from letting nature take its course. Finally, the Sande is a deliberate association (obviously part of culture), whereby women actively form norms that not only guide their own lives, but significantly shape their whole tribal community. Such cultural influence, it would seem, not only raises Sande women out of any instinctive naturalism, but also accounts for their rich measure of pride and dignity. In the Sande, they learn that being a woman is a complete way of being human, an unlimited way to the sacral powers of fertility and order.

Archaic peoples, we have seen, live in a holistic universe, where the sacred penetrates all reality. For the women of Sierra Leone, the sacred can be quite positive. Among all archaic peoples, however, sacral power has a destructive potential, for disease, natural disaster, and tribal conflict are all seen as mysterious power gone wrong. To protect themselves against such destructive waywardness, archaic tribes tend to erect taboos—constraints against certain actions thought to invite danger. One widely practiced taboo attaches to menstruating women. Many—indeed most—archaic peoples believe that men must avoid menstruating women because they emanate a dangerous sort of "woman power." (In the higher religions, too, menstruation is often thought to produce ritual uncleanness.)

The negative evaluation as dangerous or unclean seems to be a later, distorting interpretation. From what scholars can infer about the original intents of such archaic menstrual practices as seclusion from the rest of the community, the taboo represented a reverence for women's power of fertility. Among Native Americans, for instance, the menstruating woman is believed to be especially powerful because the sacred is palpably present in her. Such sacredness requires containment, lest it injure either the bearer or those she might encounter. Further, woman-power, the essence of fertility, is the polar opposite of the hunter's killing power, so woman and warrior must not meet. Were their powers to clash, the whole sacral economy could be thrown out of harmony. Then the divine forces could run amok, causing epidemic, fire, flood, loss of crops or game. Since women's fertility has an overt, menstrual sign, it was sensible to try to guard this power by taboo. The guarding however was as much positive as negative. That is, the taboo was a fence to keep fertility in for tribal benefit, as well as to keep the clash of male and female powers out.

Additionally, taboos such as this often have social benefits. The seclusion enjoined at menstruation, for instance, has given American Indian women a break from work and the demands of their husbands. Papago women call it a holiday and enjoy their power to make men hurry out of their presence. And so with other of women's taboos—they are designed to safeguard woman-power and cushion females against the strains of their hard lives. Unlike men, who must pursue power through vision quests or initiatory ordeals, American Indian women have power built into their fertile bodies. Most of the taboos shaping their lives may be read as a tribute to this power—an honoring, rather than a sign of pollution or uncleanness.

SUMMARY: ARCHAIC WOMEN'S RELIGION

We can see, then, that archaic societies have tended to provide positive religious roles for both women and men. Separate rituals and associations have regularly expressed the communities' conviction that women's natures, roles, powers, and contributions are as necessary and dignified as men's. In cultures where the dominant value has been union or harmony with the sacred, archaic woman's roles and images have naturally been held sacred. The principal focus of female sacrality (the power at which women's roles and images converged) has been fertility;

through their mytho-ritualism and shamanism, archaic societies have, with regard to women, most dramatically emphasized *motherhood*. It is true that archaic women regularly are full economic partners. It is true that many shamanize, divinize, and, especially in prehistoric groups, even rule. The base line of women's role, however, has been potential motherhood.

For if archaic women appear to have predominated in the rise of agriculture, it is probably because their wombs homologized them to Mother Earth. If they ruled ancient matrilinear groups, it was probably because they imaged the Great Mother Goddess, ruler of all that spans and grows. When women have been in danger of being discarded (for instance, through female infanticide), it has been because a tribe already had too many mouths to feed and could not risk another source of progeny. When women have been patrons of cultural arts, it has been largely because of the association of these arts with either child rearing (the association of song and poetry with enculturation) or childbirth (medical arts).

Primarily, archaic women have been vital and honored because in their cultures the fight for another generation's worth of survival has been heated. From their wombs has issued the fertility to keep humanity going. To the measure that humanity lost vivid contact with such fertility, that it distanced itself from the fertile cosmos, women tended to lose religiously based status. The story of the transition from archaic to modern culture and religion, of course, is long and complex. Through its many chapters, women have been much more than mothers. It seems fair to say, though, that the main storyline of women's exaltation and subjugation has never wandered very far from maternity. When women are accounted less human than men or relegated to providing men comfort and pleasure, it is essentially because their nurturing sort of creativity has become optional or depreciated (often at the price of great cultural loss—barbarism, bloodshed, and so on). The reader is advised to try to keep contact with this "nurturing sort of creativity" in what follows. It is not the whole cloth, but it may well be the Ariadne thread.

BIBLIOGRAPHY

Alexander, Hartley Burr. *The World's Rim*. Lincoln: University of Nebraska Press, 1967.

Brown, Joseph Epes, ed. *The Sacred Pipe*. Baltimore: Penguin Books, 1971.

Boas, Franz. *The Central Eskimo*. Lincoln: University of Nebraska Press, 1964.

Capps, Walter Holden, ed. *Seeing with a Native Eye*. New York: Harper & Row, 1976.

Eliade, Mircea. *Australian Religions*. Ithaca: Cornell University Press, 1973.

————. *Shamanism*. Princeton: University Press, 1972.

Hodgkins, Gail. "Sedna: Images of the Transcendent in an Eskimo Goddess," *Beyond Androcentrism*, Gross, Rita M., ed. Missoula: Scholars Press, 1977, pp. 305-14.

James, E.O. "Prehistoric Religion," *Historia Religionum* I, Bleeker, C. Jouco, and Widengren, Geo, eds. Leiden: E. J. Brill, 1969, pp. 23-39.

Jensen, Adolf E. *Myth and Cult among Primitive Peoples*. University of Chicago Press, 1963.

Lewis, I. M. *Ecstatic Religion*. Baltimore: Penguin Books, 1971.

MacCormack, Carol P. "Biological Events and Cultural Control," *Signs* (Autumn 1977) pp. 93-100.

Mbiti, John S. *African Religions and Philosophy*. Garden City: Doubleday, 1970.

Ortner, Sherry B. "Is Female to Male as Nature Is to Culture?" *Woman, Culture, and Society,* Rosaldo, Michelle Z., and Lamphere, Louise, eds. Stanford University Press, 1974, pp. 67-87.

Stone, Merlin. *When God Was a Woman*. New York: Dial Press, 1976.

Turnbull, Colin. *The Forest People*. New York: Simon & Schuster, 1962.

Underhill, Ruth. *Red Man's Religion*. University of Chicago Press, 1965.

THE RELIGIONS OF INDIA

Indian religion has existed for nearly six thousand years, and during its millennia the subcontinent has housed vast numbers of people (one billion are projected for the year 2000). Granted these two facts, it is not surprising that one is able to find almost any form of belief or behavior within Indian religion. Moreover, Hinduism, the umbrella life-way most Indians have walked, is incredibly diffuse. It has no central concept of God, no founder or sole prophet, no single authoritative scripture, no universal set of dogmas, no uniform moral code. Yet *dharma* ("duty"), the word most used to denote religion, is practically coextensive with Indian life. Hinduism, then, is both pervasive and extremely tolerant. It shapes all facets of Indian life, yet it countenances both primitive archaic beliefs and highly developed philosophical systems. A Hindu may worship many deities or one, by severe self-discipline or reckless abandon, in forest solitude or temple festival, through chastity or sexual orgy. Our job will be to trace how Hinduism and Indian Buddhism, its major heterodoxy, regarded and shaped Indian women through the centuries.

EARLY INDIAN RELIGION

Early Indian religion appears to be an amalgam of the religion of the Harrapans, who flourished in the Indus Valley from 4000 BCE to 2000 BCE, and that of the Aryans, who invaded the Indus Valley from the northwest around 2000 BCE. Some scholars call the fertility cults and yoga of the Harrapans "protohistoric Hinduism," while others root Hinduism in

Vedism, the Aryans' religion, as expressed in their scriptures, the Vedas. The only indisputable fact is that developed Hinduism exhibits dependencies on both these early sources.

Since the Harrapans left no literature, our knowledge of their religion is inferred from figurines, seals, and the like, which archaeologists have excavated. These suggest a central interest in fertility—in the worship of a Proto-Shiva (a three-faced god, in yogic posture, with *penis erectus,* surrounded by animals) and a Mother Goddess. The ascetic concentration on Shiva as the divinity of life-force, and the veneration of feminine power that characterizes later India, are probably both latent in Hindu Harrapan ancestry.

Generally, this early Indian concern with fertility is consonant with the facts we have reported about the typical archaic religious mind. In the Harrapan case, the interest probably was quite female-oriented, for the early Indus Valley civilization was settled and agricultural. By contrast, the Aryans were pastoral, nomadic, and warlike. It is somewhat conjectural, because of limits in the evidence, but the likelihood is that the Harrapan strain gives Hinduism its long absorption with divine "mothers." This is a term that first implied village guardians—female spirits invoked for protection. They have been worshiped mainly by the common folk, and are somewhat "negative," concerned more with warding off evil than with securing good. The female deities of later Hinduism are frequently negative, while in the Aryan charm-book called the Atharva-Veda, they are normally associated with diseases and disasters.

Mingled with devotion to the mothers is an Indian Great Goddess religion. By the time of the Vedas, it was widespread and shows female divinity under many names and forms. (Later Hinduism's interest in the female consorts of the gods is probably a survival of the early Great Goddess devotions.) The Vedas themselves are a difficult source, for they collect a vast complex of hymns, myths, rituals, magic, and philosophy from many different anonymous sources. According to tradition, these expressions of revelation were heard by holy persons lost in trancic meditation. Whatever their prehistory, they make it clear that the goddess was a rich fascination of early India.

For instance, there is Saramya, "she who runs." Saramya rushes into creation, as untamed creative will. She is a model for human life; as mother of both Death and the Asvins (twin saviors born to heal humankind's ills), she both causes problems and creates solutions. Then there is Sarama, who outwits the demons that stole away light and reestablishes cosmic order. Vedic Indians saw a trace of her celestial travels in the Milky Way. Third, the goddess appears as Sarasvati, the daughter of lightning and voice of thunder, who grants humans flashes of insight. Like the river, she rushes into human consciousness, the well-spring of intuition and creativity. In its primal layer, then, the Vedic Great Goddess religion feminizes an explosive power to generate both death and healing, cunningly restore cosmic order, and grant intuitive flashes of knowledge.

Further, the Vedas tell of Aditi, boundless Mother of All. As boundless she is androgyne: mother, father, son, all gods, being, nonbeing, whatever is or will be born. She is also Mother of Skill—particularly ritual skill needed for perfect spells and sacrifices. As Vedism became a highly priestly religion and assumed that inerrant ritual performances guaranteed cosmic order and forced the god's will, Aditi became very important. Somewhat related to this, as Vak, the goddess controlled all speech. Vak conceived the creator and gave birth without male help. She was the parthenogenic, womblike source of cosmic order, the godhead, and author, through revelation to seers and sages, of the Vedas—the eternal word.

Nor do these five titles exhaust the goddess' Vedic import. As Mother Earth, she has spawned all creatures. As Lotus, Sri, and Laksmi, she possesses and bestows beauty, power, and wealth. Mother Earth, indeed, became twin goddesses: Nirrti and Prthvi. As Nirrti she was the lap of decay, death, and the cause of order's destruction—a devouring mouth consuming all beings she mothered as Prthvi. Interestingly, Prthvi herself is always conjoined with Father Heaven. Only with him is she responsive, bounteous, nurturing.

Another duality in the Vedic Great Goddess makes her the sisters Dawn and Night. Thus, she is the blushing bride of the sun, but also dark and evil—eager to head back to cosmic dark, the realm of demons. Further, Dawn is arrogant and must be conquered by the male (originally storm) god Indra. Night is both luminous with stars (her thousand eyes) and impenetrable—a viscous stain on all she touches. The Rig Veda likens this stain to sin and guilt. Night is the goddess classically ambivalent—the soothing mother shedding soft light on her sleeping children and the fierce goddess blanketing the world in a heavy darkness that may well hide horror.

The Indian Great Goddess, therefore, is clearly multi-dimensional and highly ambivalent. To her attaches an extravagant fertility, for she is the creative source of nature, gods, humans, wit, death, order. Yet she is a dangerous mother, by turns fierce, destructive, arrogant, a source of guilt, and ineffective unless linked with Father Heaven. What is evident even from these early sources is the traditional Indian tendency to associate the female with power, energy (*shakti*), and material nature (*prakriti*)—all of which can be either benevolent or malevolent. Significantly, though, Hindu cosmology, again from prehistoric roots, makes for the female a male counterpart of spirit (*purusha*). If the female is active nature, the male spirit is "that which gives structure." Their conjunction yields structured reality, power that is controlled and therefore benevolent. The male principle is necessary if the female principle is to be fertile and good. Alone, the female principle tends to be evil and dangerous.

This theory is only clarified by the later philosophers' elaboration of matter and spirit, but it is latent in the early notions that Mother Earth needs Father Heaven in order to be bounteous, that women are soil and men their fertilizing and structuring seeds. Regularly, the moral in this configuration was driven home by the myth of Shiva and Kali. At the request of the gods, Kali killed an evil giant and his army. However, she became so excited she lost control and engaged in a frenetic dancing that threatened to shake apart the whole world. The gods could not stop her, and salvation came only when her husband Shiva lay down at her feet. Kali stopped immediately, for it is unthinkable that a devout wife would step on her husband. Popularly, the masses learned from this tale that unless husbands control their wives, the world will surely collapse.

Strangely, however, the evidence seems to indicate that the Vedic period itself was a time of comparative freedom for women. At least, Vedic women were accorded higher status than their sisters of later periods, though scholars are not clear precisely why this should have been so. One hypothesis is that earlier, the Harrapan veneration of the Great Goddess had given the feminine prestige, while later, the Aryan patriarchalism eroded women's value. On the other hand, it is argued that the Aryans brought the notion of benevolent female deities, which the Harrapan myths of the dangerous female perhaps mottled. At any rate, Vedic women apparently were fairly well educated, and they seem to have taken part in religious rituals. In some ceremonies, not only the Brahmin priest, but also his wife, had to be present (probably from a sense of androgynous wholeness). Vedic women, in addition, had rituals of their own, and the Upanishads record female philosophers such as Gargi Vacaknavi, whose penetrating questions upset the sage Yajnavalkya. Several Vedic hymns are credited to women, and some lists of scholars, poets, and teachers include feminine names.

It is true that even Vedic women were dependent on their fathers, husbands, or eldest sons, but they had property rights qualifying this dependence. In the fourth century BCE, for instance, a woman could hold a set amount of money in her own name, with her husband keeping the rest of her wealth in trust for her. At her death this money passed not to her husband or sons but to her daughters. Similarly, women of this early period were more free to travel, visit temples, attend festivals unchaperoned, and associate with men, than they were in later ages.

Nonetheless, the Vedic woman's most honored role was that of the docile wife. In fact, this role predominated in the canonical literature over that of mother. The reason for this exaltation of the docile wife no doubt lies in the ambiguity of the Mother Goddess that we noted. She is both fertile and good, evil and dangerous. The docile wife, by contrast, is safe, because controlled by her husband. Ideally, she is cheerful, prudent, chaste, honest, humble, resourceful. Always she bathes, sleeps, and eats after her husband. She is never jealous, silly, idle, or in opposition to her husband's will. Her role models in all this are Sita, who followed her husband Rama into exile, and Savitu, whose loyalty to her husband Satyavant gained his release from death. This modeling carried over to a famous medieval story. In it a wife is sitting before a fire. Her husband is asleep with his head resting in her lap. Their infant begins to crawl toward the fire. The woman remains still, lest she awaken her husband. As the baby enters the flames, the woman prays to the fire-god Agni. Agni rewards her wifely considerateness; the baby sits contented and safe in the midst of the flames until her husband awakes.

Slowly, then, Indian women were molded to wifely subservience. The good wife, indeed, is primarily docile—"half the man," source of his happiness, comfort, and courage. As such, she is cherished, feted, lavished with jewels and praise. In early times, it appears, wives had clearer rights. Just as Vedic women could study the scriptures, which later women could not, so too they had, from epic characters like Draupadi, counsel to upbraid their husbands if these failed to do dharma or wreaked injustice and suffering. Later redactors made Draupadi a hysterical shrew, but originally she was just doing her own dharma. In early religion, then, the wife was in some ways her husband's equal, not just his subordinate.

By the time of the Buddha (500 BCE), however, women were denied access to the Vedas and had no significant involvement in orthodox ritual. Between the first Vedas and the first codes of law (1500 BCE to 100 CE), Indian women's religious role steadily declined. A major reason for this was the lowering of the marriage age from fifteen or sixteen to ten, or even five. This both removed the possibility of education, and consequently of religious office, and fixed women's role to that of wife and mother.

Summarily, early Indian religion provided women some measure of status. Myths of the Great Goddess displayed the female as creator, source of order, beauty, goodness, and knowledge. Yet the Great Goddess also was considered destructive—associated with death, disease, and disaster. Male gods, though often destructive and cruel, were portrayed as more purposeful, less arbitrary and uncontrolled. Thus, there were seeds in the early religion for the later curtailment of women's freedom and repression of their rights, both religious and civil.

CLASSICAL HINDUISM AND BUDDHISM

By the end of the early period of Indian religion (about 500 BCE), there was a deposit of basic notions developed by the later philosophers and lawgivers (and epic-makers) that produce the full efflorescence we are calling classical Hinduism. If one asked for a concise statement of this system's distinctive features, it might be: belief in *karma-samsara-moksha* and acceptance of the caste system. In terms of its belief about the human condition, developed Hinduism sees us as originally ignorant of our true nature, which is oneness with the divine *(Atman)*. Because of this ignorance, we are subject to constant rebirth *(samsara)*. The level of this rebirth is determined by the quality of our previous life *(karma)*. Salvation *(moksha)* is therefore breaking the samsaric or karmic cycle by enlightenment—realization of our identity with Atman. Moksha is the central religious goal, consequently, and one's pursuit of it is significantly shaped by one's caste and sex. The most concise index of women's place in classical Hinduism is the traditional common belief that no woman of any caste could gain salvation, except in a future life, when she had been reborn as a man.

Logically, to be born a woman was the result of bad karma, for it meant that one was ineligible for moksha in this samsaric round. Tightening women's bind, orthodoxy excluded them from the most prestigious ways of accumulating good karma—study of the Vedas and meditation. Woman's salvational discipline *(yoga)*, then, was largely by way of "works." Specifically, she would advance by being a good wife, which meant by exalting her husband. So, one finds injunctions to consider one's husband a god and be his most faithful worshiper. The *Laws of Manu* (about 100 CE) instruct women to be loyal, even if their husbands are deformed, unfaithful, drunk, offensive, or debauched. To ritualize this attitude, orthodoxy suggested that the wife adore the big toe of her husband's right foot morning and evening, bathing it, offering it incense, waving lights before it.

This dedication to one's husband was supposed to continue after his death. Unlike men (and women of Vedic times), widows in the classical Hindu scheme were prohibited from remarrying. They were supposed to shun men completely, and they were conditioned to think that they had caused their husbands' deaths, devouring them through their *karmic jaw* ("their own bad karma"). In strict Hindu families, the widow was a tragic figure. She was forced to an ascetic life—sleeping on the ground, eating only one meal a day, going without honey, meat, wine, or salt, using no ointments, perfumes, or colored clothing. By medieval times, she was expected to shave her head. Since any laxity would endanger not only her own auspicious rebirth, but also her husband's, his family was vigilant in enforcing her asceticism. By medieval times, again, all of this was applied even to child brides whose marriage had never been consummated.

Manu, finally, says that a widow who remarries so violates her duty to her first husband that she disgraces herself in this life and merits rebirth as a jackal. The young widow, thus, was the Hindu triple threat—husbandless, menstruating, and a useless potential jackal. She was polluted by her closeness to death, socially burdensome, and quite likely depressed. Small wonder that so many widows chose to jump on their husbands' funeral pyres, an action which, as a further bind, was only meritorious if done from pure conjugal love. Though child marriage and *sati* ("throwing oneself on the pyre") are outlawed in modern India, the weight of tradition is such that both still occur.

The classical Hindu wife is therefore very much a shadow and unenviable type. More complicated is the role and image of the Indian woman as mother. Traditionally, her honor has devolved from the production of male children. This could win her hyperbolic praise as more divine than divinity, ten times more respectable than a father. The great philosopher Shankara writes that while a bad son might be born, there could never be a bad mother. Abstractly, motherhood was venerated. Concretely, the birth of a potential mother was a dark day. First, as noted, it was considered the result of bad karma. Second, it entailed the financial burden of a dowry, without which no daughter, up to this day, would be marriageable. It is easy to see why a little female's arrival was often announced as "nothing was born."

Still, given the nearly total subordination of the Hindu woman as wife, motherhood has been the major route to social status. As might be expected, this has heavily influenced Indian women's emotional investments, even today. Ross lists the following intensities for emotional relationships in the Indian family (the higher the figure the more intense the relationship): mother-son 115; brother-sister 90; brother-brother 75; father-son 74; husand-wife 16; sister-sister 5. The intensity of the mother-son relation shows where a Hindu woman's survival and fulfillment lay. It clearly overshadows marriage, for the low husband-wife intensity is an effect of the high mother-son—in the extended Indian family, a wife competes with her live-in mother-in-law, and loses. Also, the necessity of wifely submission to the point of adoration probably precludes the warmth and reciprocity needed for a woman's emotional fulfillment. The low sister-sister relation means that Indian sisterhood has likely been competitive and hardly powerful, while the high brother-sister relation probably means that girls have sought favor with the apples of the household's eye. Lastly, the lack of any father-daughter or mother-daughter reading seems ominously eloquent.

A further complication in Hindu motherhood is the ambiguity associated with the Great Goddess strain. As we saw, the Great Goddess is frequently called Mother—one who loves, accepts, and nurtures, but who can also hate, reject, and destroy. A goddess is never called a "wife," indicating perhaps this role's total identification with submission and powerlessness. It is, then, the mother-role that affords some potential for control and dominance, for instance, of one's own sexuality. In mythology, those goddesses who transfer control of their sexuality to their husbands are fertile and benevolent, while those who keep autonomy are labeled destructive and malevolent. The low ritual status of women relates to this estimate, for childbearing is even more polluting than menstruation. In both the Vedas and the Law Codes, role models for wives are numerous, but those for mothers are scarce. Somehow a mother is dangerously more than a docile worshiper of a husband. She has produced another person (not a "nothing," one hopes); she ex-ists, stands out, is almost something in her own right. Thus, she is threatening—yet necessary, for there must be sons. So she is highly ambiguous or ambivalent, like the Great Goddess—Female-power itself.

In 563 BCE, Siddhartha Gautama, destined to be the Buddha, was born in Northern India, a member of the warrior caste. After a comfortable youth and marriage, he was moved by the sight of suffering to seek enlightenment. Leaving his wife and infant son, later named "Fetter," he first tried to find moksha through trance, then through asceticism, and finally through philosophic meditation. (The Hindu male could legitimately cast off family ties to pursue moksha fulltime.) After six years, enlightenment came, as the insight that desire is the key to karmic entrapment. Only by giving up desire can one leave the suffering world of samsara and enter the world of fulfillment (nirvana).

Buddha ("the Enlightened One") gathered a band of disciples and began to preach this new insight. In essence, he preached the Four Noble Truths: all reality is suffering; the key to suffering is desire; desire can be stopped; the way to stop desire is to follow the Eightfold Path [right views, right intentions, right speech, right actions, right livelihood, right effort, right mindfulness, and right concentration]. The best context or atmosphere in which to follow the Eightfold Path is the Buddhist monastic community (Sangha), and it is here that we find much of Buddhism's implications for Indian women.

Whereas Hinduism limited moksha to men of upper caste, Buddha preached to all who would hear, holding that nirvana is within reach of anyone willing to live out the Four Noble Truths. With this will, one could take monastic vows, the core of which has been the Three Jewels: "I take refuge in the Buddha, the Dharma, and the Sangha." Having preached to women, Buddha had to deal with their applications to the Sangha. Some sources, which may well represent later monk-editors, assert that he admitted women reluctantly, moaning that they would shorten the lifespan of pure religion.

Still, whatever the reluctance, opening Buddhist religious life to women gave them a liberating option beyond marriage and motherhood. It meant a sort of career, and a chance for greater independence. No longer need a girl and her family concentrate solely on gathering a dowry and arranging a wedding. Indeed, Hindu child marriages were sure to be viewed as reprehensible. Concretely, Buddhist women appear to have traveled freely to wherever Buddha preached. They were praised for their fidelity to dharma and their financial generosity. One can see analogues to the early Christian women, for these first female Buddhist disciples taught, preached, gave hospitality, time, and money to the fresh cause.

Moreover, by offering an alternative to marriage, Buddhism inevitably gave women more voice in their marriage decisions, and then in their conjugal lives. In fact, a Buddhist view of marriage approached seeing the spouses as equal. The husband owed the wife respect, courtesy, faithfulness, relinquishing of authority, and adornment. The wife owed the husband duties well done, hospitality to their parents, faithfulness, watchfulness over his earnings, skill, and industry. One concrete way that a Buddhist wife shared authority was in choosing their children's careers. Both parents' consent, for instance, was needed for a child to enter the monastery. Further, married women could inherit, and they could manage their property without interference. Widows were not required or even expected to become recluses, and sati would have been abhorrent to a religion that condemned animal sacrifice, murder, and suicide. Finally, Buddhist widows could enter the Sangha, where they might find very helpful religious companionship, or they could stay in the world, remarry, inherit, and manage their own affairs.

By the time of the canonical literature (second century BCE), however, this positive view of women began to abate and one notes the beginning of a fateful theme that women are dangerous temptations. The likely source of this theme was the pressure of male celibacy. Many monks were former house-holders, for whom wives' being out of sight did not necessarily mean their being out of imagination. In the Jataka tales that sprang up about the Buddha's early lives, one finds an emphasis on female perfidy. Women (often pictured as ugly, blind, and wretched) are shown betraying fathers, husbands, sons, and ascetics (pictured as noble, loyal, generous, and holy) because of their unruly sexual needs. The motivation clearly seems to be to shore up males' resistance to libidinal urges.

Sadly, Buddhist literature came to make women an obstacle to monks' perfection and painted females as being sexually ravenous, greedy, envious, stupid, and generally repulsive. Monastic virtue, concomitantly, became less and less a good life, more and more a matter of sexual abstinence. This spilled over to marriage as well, making the virtuous wife the chaste wife, which entailed curtailing wives' freedom and considering the unfettered woman a religious menace. Eventually, then, the Buddhist canonical literature came to mirror the Hindu. The good wife is totally submissive, uses only sweet words, honors all her husband's wishes, and obeys his every command.

Within the Sangha, too, nuns' position deteriorated. Unlike men, women needed their spouses' consent to join the monastery. Individually and collectively, nuns were considered subservient to monks. Only monks could interpret dharma, and nunneries needed a monk's presence during the stable rainy season. Women did have some say in running their houses, and they were always thought capable of enlightenment and nirvana. Their political impotence is indicated, however, in the common view that a woman could not create a schism (that is, she would not have the influence to form a new sect). Moreover, nuns continued to be offered the palliative that good works would bring them rebirth as men and as a result, better opportunities for salvation in the next life. As fortifying examples, they were given the Buddha's mother, who died seven days after his birth and was reborn as a male god, and the virtuous maiden who, by "cultivating the thoughts of a man," was reborn as the son of a god. The story circulated that Buddha himself had never suffered the indignity of a female birth, and many doubted that any woman could herself become a buddha, an absolutely enlightened one. As Buddhism developed, women gained some religious rights, but they continued to be primarily "no-men."

It is clear that the Sangha's stress on celibacy greatly contributed to the view of women as personal obstacles to monkish perfection, but what caused women to be seen as cosmic obstacles, retarding the spiritual progress of mankind? Falk (1974) suggests the familiar equation of "female" with "fertility." Free association, begun among archaic Indians, easily could yield woman = sex, offspring, motherhood, nurturing, abundance, plentiful crops, fertile flocks. Picking this up, some Buddhist authors showed women as sexually insatiable, never tiring of intercourse and childbearing. So great are their needs that they should not be held responsible if they take any means to satisfy them. Early conservative Buddhism (Theravadin) linked their desire and productive becoming with samsara, the realm of change and endless redistribution of the life-force. Since samsara was the enemy and trap, so too was femaleness. Thus women took on symbolic force as epitomizing karmic bonds. In the story of Buddha's encounter with the daughters of Mara, the god of desire and worldliness, the faithful were read out this symbolism in cautionary form. To prevent Buddha from reaching enlightenment, which would threaten his samsaric sway, Mara sent his three beautiful daughters Desire, Pleasure, and Passion. It was by withstanding their seduction that the Perfect One entered into nirvana and gained saving truth—by triumphing over the world of allure and the senses, the world of women! As Hinduism ultimately stigmatized women as cosmic matter, so Buddhism finally stigmatized them as bondage.

Something commonly Indian infected both Hinduism and Buddhism with a dark and deeply misogynistic strain. Unless a woman is neutralized by marriage to a controlling man, Hindu imagination conjures up for her such images as the snake, death, the underworld, hell's entrance, the prostitute, the adulteress. As Manu, the classical law-giver, expressed it, women are simply wicked:

It is the nature of women to seduce men . . . ; for that reason the wise are never unguarded . . . For women are able to lead astray in (this) world not only a fool, but even a learned man, and (to make) him a slave of desire and anger. One should not sit in a lonely place with one's mother, sister, or daughter; for the senses are powerful, and master even a learned man.

(II:213-15)

Therefore, Manu concludes, it is a fixed rule that women are as corrupt as falsehood itself.

Classical Buddhism paralleled Manu's misogynism by embroidering the episode of Siddhartha's leaving home to seek enlightenment, with the following denigrating legend: Beautiful dancing girls were performing for the Buddha-to-be, but he fell asleep. The women therefore shrugged their shoulders and curled up themselves. When Siddhartha awoke, he saw the dancing girls sleeping: saliva trickled from their mouths; they were covered with sweat; some ground their teeth; some snored; the garments of some were in disarray, "so that they repulsively showed their private parts." This sight so filled Siddhartha with disgust that he likened the banquet hall to a charnel ground full of corpses.

In this vein, monks were encouraged by eminent masters of meditation, such as Buddhaghosa, to concentrate on the repulsiveness of the body. As an example, they were given the story of the monk who happened upon a woman "adorned and beautified like a heavenly maiden." The woman had just quarreled with her husband, and seeing the monk, she desired him. She laughed aloud to get his attention. Startled, the monk looked up, and seeing her teeth, which reminded him of bones, he was filled with disgust. Immediately, he reached enlightenment. It is not surprising that the following dialogue, ascribed to Buddha and his favorite disciple Ananda, could be found credible:

"How are we to conduct ourselves, Lord, with regard to womankind?"

"As not seeing them, Ananda."

"But if we should see them, what are we to do?"

"No talking, Ananda."

"But if they should speak to us, Lord, what are we to do?"

"Keep awake, Ananda."

By the eighth or ninth centuries of the Common Era, Buddhism had largely been absorbed by Hinduism in India and had transported its real life to other lands. The movement that dominated Indian religion after the full articulation of these two traditions into classical form, however, undercut their differences and reached back to pre-Aryan (Harrapan) roots. This was devotionalism, in its various forms of bhakti, shaktism, and tantra. It was a people's movement, rather than the religion of priests, philosophers, or monks, and it made sizable impacts on Indian women. For example, as is frequenty the case with popular religious movements, Indian devotionalism ignored distinctions of caste and sex. Most of its groups were even open to outcasts, and they admitted women as equal devotees of the gods. In fact, since it was democratic, emotional, and did not require much learning, devotionalism was, in the eyes of many, especially suited to women.

There were philosophers, such as Ramanuja, who tried to justify devotionalism, but the masses who poured out their hearts before statues of Shiva or the Buddha needed no philosophical reasons. Disputes over the nature of moksha or nirvana could mean little to an illiterate shopkeeper or the mother of a dying child. Yet both understood pain, love, and sorrow. Hence, both could respond to the stories of a Shiva whose penances and fastings kept the universe on its course. Similarly, both could be drawn to icons depicting the compassionate Buddha and celebrate his birthday joyously. Like ourselves, Indians have always found it easier to love "someone with skin on" than to follow abstract theological debates.

In form, Indian devotionalism varies from the simple gesture of putting flower petals on Gandhi's tomb at Raj–Ghat to elaborate village festivals. A capsule way of dealing with female aspects of devotionalism in Buddhism is to study the place of Lady Wisdom *(Prajnaparamita)* in the Mahayana philosophy and the way women were treated in the tantric rites of the

Vajrayana sects. For Hindu devotionalism, we can concentrate on what bhakti and tantra meant for Hindu women.

Mahayana Buddhism arose from a schism that occurred about two hundred years after Gautama's death. It was the more liberal school, stressing that there is nothing in human experience that cannot be used for enlightenment, because in time all things are sure to reveal their emptiness. Wisdom, therefore, sees a oneness in all reality. It goes beyond divisions of "this world" and "the next world." Lady Wisdom is the personification of the realization that all things are one because no things are fully satisfying. Zen, which depends on this Mahayana stress on oneness, has expressed it in striking *koans*—illogical sayings designed to jolt the mind out of its dualisms. So, for instance, the master may urge the disciple to concentrate on the sound of one hand clapping, or on what your face was before your parents were born. What is intriguing for our purposes is that Mahayana makes this Prajnaparamita, this Supreme Wisdom, feminine.

Because Prajnaparamita, like nirvana, cannot be imagined or conceived, it is not normally portrayed as a goddess, though later some devotional sects so picture it. Rather, it is the gracious, ladylike insight that almost maternally rescues poor humans from their ignorance, suffering, karma and rebirth. In other words, it is a wisdom supremely compassionate—supremely full of the *mahakaruna*, the Buddhist equivalent of charity or religious love, which motivates buddhas and bodhisattvas to labor for the salvation through enlightenment of all living things. In this way, Prajnaparamita is "the mother of all buddhas," their source, nurturer, and sustainer.

Psychologically, one can only marvel at the intuitions behind this feminization of Buddhist wisdom. How better to encourage people in the midst of trying to cast off all worldly securities, so as to live by no-thing-ness, than to assure them that the final quality of reality and enlightenment is a gentle supportive compassion? Unlike the ambivalent Hindu Mother Goddess, the Prajnaparamita is pure liberation, "herself" empty of anything clinging or defiled. Thus she can be defense, shelter, and protection from the samsaric storms, the suffering of worldly striving and desire.

In this way she has gentled many to let go their fears and jump into the enlightenment-abyss. Like the bird pushed from the nest, the soul that responds to Lady Wisdom will neither crash to earth, nor rest on any visible support. It will use its wings to fly—to live clear-eyed, realistically, finding an empty nirvana in the midst of samsara.

Hinduism's mother-figures, we saw, have been ambivalent—necessary but dangerous, loved but also feared. One metaphysical explanation for the difference of the Prajnaparamita is that Hinduism split matter and spirit, while Mahayana Buddhism tended to keep them whole. Philosophical Hinduism has tended to see matter, prakriti, which is considered feminine, as binding. Spirit, purusha, considered masculine, must free itself from matter if it is to achieve moksha. Hence, the Hindu Great Goddess is like Rudolf Otto's "Holy"—a Mystery both fearsome and alluring. She is attractive for her fecundity and care, but her binding possessiveness, her material here-and-nowness, is terrifying. Culturally, the drive to a purely spiritual state of liberation made Hinduism consider the feminine as a beguilement or trap.

Mahayana avoids this metaphysical stigmatizing of the feminine, since it does not place matter and spirit in opposition. Rather, they are coordinated and codependent. Faith in Prajnaparamita will lead one to see that both matter and spirit, as normally conceived, are passing, impermanent, unworthy of religious desire. True liberation, truly unconditioned existence, nirvana, is beyond them both. At the heart of its world-view, then, Buddhism sought a holism that reflected, in philosophical terms, the balance and respect for the feminine that the archaic religious mind expressed through androgyny.

Practically, the influence of this Mahayana intuition was that it viewed women less negatively, with fewer figures like "temptress" or "trap," than did the more traditionally Indian, even "Hindu" schools of the conservative Theravadins. Relatedly, Mahayana placed less emphasis on monastic life and celibacy, upgrading the laity and sanctioning the possibility of enlightenment within marriage. This led to viewing women more as partners of men, just as it led to less fear and depreciation of "the world." The world, samsara, was to be faced and understood, not fled or rejected. Nirvana lies in the midst of samsara. Enlightenment is an empty-fullness at the core of eating as well as fasting, sexual intercourse as well as abstinence. As one of the prime Prajnaparamita texts puts it, "Those who are certain that they have got safely out of this world are unfit for full enlightenment."

Tantrism, in both Hinduism and Buddhism, is a mixture of mysticism, magic, yoga, and devotionalism. The word itself refers to the manuals that explain the rituals that Indian religion developed from this mixture. Buddhist tantra utilizes the Mahayana belief that nirvana and samsara are the same. Since all reality is empty, nothing is forbidden or taboo. Rather, anything can trigger enlightenment, if it is used with proper discipline. Specifically, tantrists, under strict obedience to their guru, could engage in such socially proscribed activities as drinking wine, eating meat, and sexual intercourse. They were not to engage in them for pleasure, which would have increased karma and entrapment, but as a means of liberation. For instance, where the celibate renounced sexual intercouse in order to free himself from desire and karma, the tantrist renounced the celibate's renunciation, in order to affirm the emptiness of all virtue or desire for desirelessness. As one might expect, it was this ritual use of sex *(maithuna)* that was capital for tantrism's influence on women.

To begin at the top, we should note that Prajanaparamita became a central figure in Buddhist tantra. In effect, she became the Goddess of Wisdom. Her male equivalent was Upaya, Skill in Means. Symbolically, the union of Wisdom and Means is a union of intuition and action—of the seeing and doing which Buddhists collocate with enlightenment. By a quasi-magical imitation or parallelism, tantrism held that an adept could gain the union of the two deities Prajnaparamita and Upaya in sexual intercourse. Imaginatively or physically, the human couple, in their sexual play, mirror the divine cosmic principles in their interaction. Perfect union, achieved with perfect control of the senses, would bring the adept right to the heart of enlightenment's androgyny.

In Hindu and Taoist (native Chinese) sexual yoga, it is clear that the female is largely used for the male's spiritual advance. In these traditions the male learns to withhold his semen while bringing the female to orgasm. The reasoning is that thereby he retains his own vital force (associated with semen) and takes the female's. Things appear to have been understood somewhat differently among the Buddhist tantrists. Since they held wisdom and means as both necessary, the female could not be used onesidedly. There was some inclination, in other words, to have the partners develop a mutual use or service, in imitation of the cooperation between Prajnaparamita and Upaya.

In the Vajrayana ("Thunderbolt") school of Buddhism, which was especially influential in Tibet, tantric convictions led to women becoming gurus or masters. Such women were called *siddhas,* and they were believed to be perfectly enlightened. Since Vajrayana tradition depended upon transmission through a line of masters, the siddhas had a quasi "institutional" importance. One of the striking features of the siddhas' teaching was that, pushing Mahayana notions of emptiness, they counseled their followers to stop thinking of themselves as anything definite enough to be bound by social convention. Their "crazy wisdom" was expressed through bizarre and eccentric behavior, as well as through trampling on social taboos. In addition, Vajrayana developed the notion of *Taras,* goddesses or savioresses who were consorts of the buddhas, and this had great influence on popular piety.

Nonetheless, the inbuilt sexism of Indian social formation made it difficult for women to become gurus, even in Vajrayana. This is illustrated in the case of Laksminkara, a famous siddha born in Northwest India in the eighth century CE. Since Northwest India was at that time a stronghold of Vajrayana, Laksminkara had access to tantric teachings from early childhood. Because she was of royal blood, however, she was betrothed at age seven to the Hindu ruler of a neighboring kingdom. For nine years, Laksminkara remained in her family home, studying the tantras and being initiated, until it came time for her marriage. Then everything started to go wrong. Her reception at her husband's castle was very cold, because the harem, as well as the general populace, resented her as a Buddhist outsider. As she waited outside the castle, Laksmin-kara saw the royal hunting party returning with their catch, a newly slain deer. This so shocked her Buddhist soul that she fainted dead away. Upon reviving, she gave away her dowry and all her jewels. Then she locked herself in a room, to go naked and feign insanity. After many tribulations, she wandered in abject poverty for seven years, all the while pretending to be insane, a favorite tantric ruse for rejecting common values. Eventually her suffering won her deep enlightenment and many disciples, among them her former husband and her brother. Much in Laksminkara's life story, no doubt, is legendary, but it testifies to the possibility of a female tantric guru.

Meanwhile, within the dominant strands of Hindu devotion-alism, the Great Goddess was returning to the fore. From about 1000 CE, Hindu tantrism made a great deal of Devi. Since Devi just means goddess, it was shorthand for Durga, Kali, Uma, Vak, Parvati, and the other female deities who went back to earliest times. Like Buddhist tantrism, the Hindu variety stressed a complete break with social conventions, especially by employ-ing ritual intercourse as a means to moksha. Much of this ritual intercourse was modeled on the union of divine couples, especially that of Shiva and Devi. Because Devi was Shiva's consort *(shakti),* Hindu tantrism of this type is called shaktism. Followers would meet in secret at night, consume forbidden meat and wine, and engage in ritual intercourse. In theory, this was not an orgy. Indeed, years of study and yogic training were supposed to prepare the male disciples to perform all these acts of license without sensual gratification. In the preparatory prayers, the disciples were reminded that their female partners were not ordinary women, but rather Shakti herself. If they thought otherwise, they would be guilty of impurity and would earn bad karma.

The data on women's roles in Hindu tantrism are mixed. It is clear that they could join most sects, contrary to orthodox Hindu movements, and sometimes it appears that they could gain influence as ascetics or gurus. On the other hand, much in the ritual literature suggests that the ordinary situation made women instruments of men's spiritual progress—that they were valued mainly for concretizing shakti-power. Within the symbolism of this shakti-power itself, one finds indications that the ancient Hindu ambivalence about the feminine reached into even the tantric movements. As Durga, the Devi upholds heaven by her chastity, yet delights in wine, meat, and animal sacrifice. As Uma, she seduces a buffalo demon, slays him, and drinks his blood. As Kali, "The Dark One," she wears a garland of skulls and drinks her victims' blood. In most forms, she is dangerous, impetuous, sexy, violent, vengeful. This is all in such contrast to the normal Hindu wife, whose only route to moksha was submission to her husband, that it seems mainly to be male fantasy written cosmically. In fact, most of Devi's followers have been male. Female-power, then, was more in the service of male satisfaction than it was a positive symbolization of Hindu women's religious dignity. Devi was the active power complementing Shiva's passive, pure intelligence—a power *of* Shiva. Though Hindu tantrism opened to women, and was a force against such social forms of misogynism as widow-burning, it kept the traditional dualism that ranked spirit-male above matter-female. At any rate, Hindu tantra always remained a rather marginal, esoteric movement, without much popular impact.

It was *bhakti,* theistic love-religion, therefore, that shaped most Hindu women and most protested dualism, caste distinctions, and sexual prejudice. In essence, bhakti taught that moksha can come through intense, emotional dedication to a personal deity. The deity could be female or male, but the most popular ones were Shiva and Visnu, the latter especially in his incarnation as Krishna. This squares with the general bhakti view that divinity is male and humanity is female (which makes devotion a love-union on the model of marriage). A more romantic model lies in the stories of Krishna's dalliance with the *gopis* ("cowgirls"). If the devotee loves her god fiercely enough, she will be freed of egocentric, karma-producing concerns. In raptured union with the god, beguiled, as the gopis were by the teasing Krishna, she will have a foretaste of moksha—the unconditioned state philosophers described as: being, bliss, and awareness. The great advantage of this devotionalism, of course, is that anyone can love. It does not require great learning or leisure. One need not meditate or go ascetic or curry favor with priests. True, much bhakti seems to have degenerated to trashy and unrealistic emotionalism—to a kind of Hindu "true confessions"—but, on the other hand, deep thinkers and impeccable saints have supported it, for they have seen that few forces are more powerful in transforming human lives, or more central symbols of ultimate Mystery, than is wholehearted love.

Politically, it is to bhakti's credit that women were accounted as eligible for salvation, and that in some sects women were given the sacred thread (sign of rebirth), allowed to make pilgrimages and vows to their chosen deity, and encouraged to education. Bhakti's preoccupation with emotional love fostered poetry and songwriting (many sects spread their teachings through religious troubadours), much of which was done by bhaktas devoted to Shiva or Krishna. These women might write, "I love the Beautiful One with no bond, no fear, no clan, no land." Their songs mixed erotic longing and selfless commitment. Frequently the devotees scorned social conventions, much as tantrists did, in order to show their complete dedication. Belonging to a divine lover, they argued, made spouses, family, possessions, or even self-respect worthless.

It is likely, of course, that social oppression contributed to many bhaktas' intensity, as the excess in some of their emotionalism suggests. For instance, many marriages must have been emotionally intolerable. They would have been arranged for reasons of social status and often involved great differences in age. As the previously cited study of emotional relations within the modern Indian family suggests, spouses often gave one another little emotional fulfillment. On the other hand, young girls were, and still are, encouraged to romanticize marriage and fantasize lush feelings, but today films have replaced folk tales and poetry. So bhakti religion often appeared as a blessed, legitimate escape from an all too human earthly spouse to a perfect divine lover. Mahadevi, who wrote influential poems to Shiva in the twelfth century CE, complained bitterly about her in-laws and unfaithful husband—"no god, this man." She would have her revenge by cuckolding him with Shiva. The poem clearly has allegorical levels, with husband and in-laws representing karmic ties. Still, it also expresses the solid base that bhakti had in sexist injustice and females' social oppression. Since one of religion's central functions is to save adherents from life's deadends, it is no denigration of bhakti to point out that it gave many neglected Hindu wives their only chance for an unrestricted love.

Moreover, the *Bhagavad-Gita,* India's most revered religious work, was a strong sanction for bhakti. It has Krishna say that all who love him will be saved. In fact, one of the great "revelations" that the Gita discloses is that Krishna himself loves his devotees, making him a far cry from an unmovable Brahman or Atman, the philosophers' divinity. As well, bhakti often joined Krishna with his consort Radha, as its Shivite sects joined Shiva with Parvati. The result was a certain androgynization of Hindu divinity, even to the point of iconography in which both Shiva and Visnu were hermaphrodites—half male and half female. In this way, beauty could join strength, tender join powerful, matter join spirit, femininity join the recesses of divinity. Bhakti poetry on occasion mirrors such iconography, tending to disdain gender distinctions in both the human and the divine spheres. Thus Radha speaks of her love with Krishna in words such as, "Neither was he a man nor I a woman. Love blended us together into a perfect whole." Similarly, poems to Shiva insist that "self" is more than beard or breast, whiskers or long hair. For those with ears to hear, then, bhakti bore seeds of a sexual equality founded in divinity itself.

In modern India, one finds a sort of living religious museum that preserves most of the emphases that six thousand years of history have generated. There is still polytheism and animism, high speculation and wild shaktism, as well as colorations produced by long contact with Christianity and Islam, and recent contact with scientific secularism and Marxism. Christianity, however, though it may have reached India as early as the first century, has today only about two percent of the population. McGrath suggests that Christian women missionaries did a great deal to improve Indian women's station during the late nineteenth and twentieth centuries, especially through the Protestant missionary policy of providing high quality colleges for women. Islam, which dominated India politically from 1200 to 1700, brought the degradations of the harem and the Qur'anic bases of sexism. Hindu bhakti did find in *Sufism* ("Islamic devotionalism") a soulmate supporting a love-mysticism, and the Western influences, especially those under the British rule, have changed Indian conceptions of science, education, and political organization. Both British and Muslim rulers opposed widow-burning, but Islam brought veiling and greater segregation of the sexes. The British opposed these, along with child marriage, prostitution, female infanticide, and the prohibition of widows' remarriage.

Gandhi, the architect of independence, made women's emancipation a cornerstone of his politico-religious program. More than seventy thousand women took part in his famous march against the Salt Tax, and many of the legal gains women have made recently stem from his inspiration. Among these gains have been the 1949 Constitution's forbidding of sex discrimination and extending the vote to women; the Marriage Act of 1955 that ended polygamy and polyandry, permitted divorce, and set minimum marriage ages of fifteen for girls and eighteen for boys; and the abolition of prostitution in 1956, and the dowry in 1961.

Unfortunately, these laws have far from overturned conventional practices. Fifteen years after the dowry legislations, for instance, an upper-caste family with a well-educated and well-employed son could still command a dowry of $10,000, plus a car, TV, or refrigerator. A rural family might expect for a good "catch" perhaps $2000 and a sewing machine or transistor radio. Frequently poor families go into debt for generations in order to secure an upwardly mobile son-in-law. In a land where ninety percent of the marriages are still arranged, hundreds of millions of women continue to be told that they are worth the dowry price they can muster. Because of this, and the pressure of living with in-laws, female suicide is a major problem. In 1975, New Delhi alone recorded eighty-nine suicides of wives, and Indian newspapers regularly report stories of "accidental" deaths, which probably were murders by husbands particularly galled by an inadequate dowry. Finally, these poisonous effects of the dowry continue to foster the belief that the birth of a daughter is due to bad karma, which in turn leads to a "benign" neglect of female children and a high rate of female infant mortality. As well, the desire for sons forces many Indian women into otherwise unwanted pregnancies.

Modern India, thus, is in a crosscurrent of tradition and new aspirations. A woman may attend the university, but still be expected to be a docile wife and bear many sons. Similarly, she may still face the dilemma of being the spouse of a *sannyasi* or holy man—a householder who renounces all his possessions, including his wife, in order to pursue moksha. When such a man chooses his new path, he undergoes a ritual death and rebirth, taking a new name and shedding all his previous worldly ties and obligations. He is free. His wife is caught—is she his spouse or his widow? Often she is neither, for he may acknowledge no relationship to her at all. Even today a husbandless wife is a tragic figure, for Indian society continues to be geared for home and family. The devoted wife must therefore face the anguish of either opposing her husband's pursuit of spiritual perfection or accepting her own social and religious diminishment (religious, because her normal way to good karma is by serving her husband).

One partial solution to this dilemma is for the wife herself to become a *sannyasini,* and this illumines the family lives of several eminent Indian religious leaders. Being a sannyasini entails celibate cohabitation. In effect, the ascetic husband receives the full attention and care of his wife. The ascetic wife receives the privilege of giving him such attention and care. Also, she will be "his" for seven more lives, unless he reaches moksha and is no longer reborn! Meanwhile, even this cohabitation depends on the husband's good pleasure. Since his motive is getting rid of obligations as often as it is sincere religious ambition, he frequently will not allow his wife to accompany him. Tradition sanctions some of his freedom, too, for the great philosopher Ramanuja is said to have been annoyed by his wife's strict orthodoxy, sent her packing to her parents, and become a sannyasi without her knowledge or consent. Somewhat similarly, Mahatma Gandhi undertook celibacy as part of his self-discipline campaign to free India from British rule, without giving his wife Kasturba much say in the matter. The mystic and theologian Ramakrishna married but refused to consummate the bond, though he did show his wife great love and affection. On the whole, then, this sannyasi tradition remains an ultimate way for men to defect on their conjugal obligations, and an ultimate sign of women's inferior religious status.

Ramakrishna's influence on modern Indian religious imagination makes his view of women a good case study with which to close our survey of traditional ambivalences. He warned that "women and gold" keep one from enlightenment, and since women are a main cause of desiring gold, they become samsara itself. To talk at length with a women, then, was equated with carnal intercourse. On the other hand, Ramakrishna's own religious life was dominated by the Great Goddess, to the point of obsession and seizure. His major mystical experience was a vision of Kali, the Dark Mother, and he underwent tantric initiation from a female guru. When he prayed to Krishna he "became" a woman, dressing for six months in female clothing and imitating feminine gestures. (Some of his followers claim that during this time he began to menstruate.) All this is from the man who said that an ascetic enjoying contact with a woman is like a man swallowing the spittle he had expectorated. Up to very recent times, then, woman-power in the abstract has been powerful and divine for India. In the concrete, it has been feared, despised, and regularly consigned to inferior human status.

BIBLIOGRAPHY

Basham, A.L. *The Wonder That Was India.* New York: Grove Press, 1954.
Buhler, G., trans. *The Laws of Manu.* Delhi: Motilal Banarsidass, 1971.

Conze, Edward. *Buddhist Meditation*. New York: Harper Torchbooks, 1956.

Dandekar, R.N. "Hinduism," *Historia Religionum II*, Bleeker, C. Jouco, and Widengren, Geo, eds. Leiden: E. J. Brill, 1971, pp. 237-345.

Falk, Nancy. "An Image of Woman in Old Buddhist Literature: The Daughters of Mara," *Women and Religion*, rev. ed., Plaskow, Judith, and Romero, Joan Arnold, eds. Missoula: Scholars Press, 1974, pp. 105-12.

———. "Draupadi and the Dharma," *Beyond Androcentrism*, Gross, Rita M., ed. Missoula: Scholars Press, 1977, pp. 89-114.

Hejit, Alaka. "Wife or Widow? The Ambiguity of the Status of the Renounced Wife of a Sannyasi." Paper delivered at the American Academy of Religion, San Francisco, December 1977.

Hopkins, Thomas J. *The Hindu Religious Tradition*. Encino, Cal.: Dickenson Publishing Co., 1971.

Horner, I. B. *Women Under Primitive Buddhism*. New York: Dutton, 1930.

Kramrisch, Stella. "The Indian Great Goddess," *History of Religions* (May 1975) pp. 235-65.

Macy, Joanna Rogers. "Perfection of Wisdom: Mother of All Buddhas," *Beyond Androcentrism*, Gross, Rita M., ed. Missoula: Scholars Press, 1977, pp. 315-33.

McGrath, Sister Albertus Magnus, O. P. *What a Modern Catholic Believes about Women*. Chicago: Thomas More Association, 1972.

Organ, T. W. *Hinduism: Its Historical Development*. Woodbury: Barron's Educational Series, 1974.

Ramanuja, A. K., trans. *Speaking of Siva*. Baltimore: Penguin Books, 1973.

Robinson, Richard H., and Johnson, Willard L. *The Buddhist Religion*, 2nd ed. Encino, Cal.: Dickenson Publishing Co., 1977.

Ross, Aileen D. *The Hindu Family in Its Urban Setting*. Toronto Universiy Press, 1961.

Sharma, Arvind. "Ramakrisna Paramahamsa: A Study in a Mystic's Attitude Towards Women," *Beyond Androcentrism*, Gross, Rita M., ed. Missoula: Scholars Press, 1977, pp. 115-24.

Wadley, Susan. "Women in the Hindu Tradition," *Signs* (Autumn 1977) pp. 113-25.

EAST ASIAN RELIGIONS

The millenial cultures of China and Japan have been shaped by several religious traditions. Confucianism and Taoism are native to China, while Buddhism, imported in the first century CE, soon was transformed and given a distinctly Chinese character. Recently, Chinese Communism, which one may call a quasi-religion, has been changing both Confucian-based tradition and Marxism. Similarly, during its shorter historical course, Japan has articulated its archaic notions into Shinto, adapted Buddhism, and created "new religions" designed for modern minds. Yet the constant, or core foundation, for East Asian culture has been Confucian ethics, because these most shaped family life and government.

Of course, even to distinguish different East Asian religions is misleading, for neither Chinese nor Japanese have thought in terms of separation or opposition among their different cultural ways. So there is the Chinese proverb, "In office a Confucian, in retirement a Taoist, in death a Buddhist." Japanese often are married by a Shinto priest and buried in a Buddhist ceremony. To claim a certain centrality for Confucianism, then, is not to deny that it has interacted with several other visions.

NATIVE CHINESE VIEWS OF WOMEN

Both Confucianism and Taoism, China's native traditions, draw on archaic, prehistoric beliefs. Interestingly, there is evidence that these beliefs were shaped by a matriarchal social structure. Chinese mythology, for instance, speaks of a Great Ancestress who held sway first in her own right, and then as mother of the hero. In addition, there are indications that before kingship became the rule, power was in the hands of a royal couple who shared political, domestic, and religious roles alike. On the basis of what we have seen for other cultures, this would suggest a Mother Goddess substratum in Chinese pre-history and a strong sense of the androgyne. Later theory that nature is a composite of *yin* ("female") and *yang* ("male"), as well as feminine overtones to the *Tao* ("cosmic and social Way"), may well be rooted in such a substratum.

What is certain is that the earliest formation of Chinese beliefs includes these notions of yin/yang and Tao. It also includes animism ("a reverence for spirits"), and ancestor veneration. Animism seems to stem from the Chinese strong feeling of dependence upon the uncontrollable forces that guide the world. Its tendency, therefore, is to find everything to be alive; rocks, trees, rivers, and mountains have spirits, as surely as animals and humans. Mother Earth was a quite literal title. The sacrality from which things issued had to be preeminently alive. Ancestor veneration—ritually honoring the dead, in order to secure blessings and avert evil—is but a dimension of animism, for the dead continue to be close by as spirits, while their bodies have returned to Mother Earth.

By the time of the legends on which Confucius (551-479 BCE) drew, male rule had become China's dominant political organization. The Master's heroes and villains are therefore largely male. It is reported, however, that he once found a version of the *I Ching* ("Book of Divination"), in which feminine power had priority over male, but this does not seem to have greatly influenced his interpretation of the past. Rather, the religious elements that Confucius did use to create his version of the ancients' Way stressed order and reserve, largely because these were the needs of a confused and warring time. As well, they were Confucius' views of past heroes' nobility: "I have 'transmitted what was taught to me without making up anything of my own.' I have been faithful to and loved the Ancients" (*Analects,* 7:1).

Confucius' "past" was a golden age of harmony—in the

cosmos, among different peoples, between individuals, within the self. Tao reigned, yin and yang were in balance, nature was at peace. To restore such harmony a society needed rulers who would embody and impose the old ethics. Confucius never found a ruler who would put his principles into effect, so he contented himself with training young men of promise. Of women he is reported to have said, "Closeness makes them hard to handle, distance makes them moody." His training may be summarized in four concepts: *li, hsiao, jen,* and *Tao.*

Li is correct behavior and ritual protocol, based on five superior/inferior relationships: ruler/subject; father/son; husband/wife; oldest sons/younger sons; elders/juniors. Hsiao is filial piety, which holds these five relationships together. By hsiao one serves one's parents in life, mourns and venerates them in death, honors one's ruler, and shows deference to all superiors. Jen is Confucius' highest virtue: humaneness, simple goodness, love. It is what keeps the five relationships from becoming tyrannical or servile. Last, there is Tao, the way to harmony. For Confucius, Tao meant the social propriety, the graceful (because attuned to nature) correctness, that the ancient heroes had discovered. The China that took guidance from this master, then, would be a family-oriented, highly ordered, and status-conscious society, whose highest good was stable harmony.

While the status of women in China down the centuries was shaped by Confucian, Taoist, and Buddhist views, Confucianism was by far the most influential and misogynistic. As the husband/wife relationship epitomized it, women were simply inferior to men. For instance, though Chinese society was rooted in ancestor veneration, no daughter could offer rites for her parents. Hence the saying, "The most excellent daughter is not worth a splay-footed son." Also, the dire poverty of many periods forced not a few parents to balance society's need for future mothers against a present excess of mouths to feed. Five sons to two daughters was the ratio often targeted, and this led to endemic female infanticide. Moreover, if the girl-infant survived, she might well be sold, since she would have to leave home when she married anyway. "Rearing marriages," where the child lived with her future in-laws, were but a variant on this theme. Little wonder that the common term for girls could translate "slave-girl."

While wealthy women were largely spared these pains, their marital lot was seldom easy. In fact, upper-class urban women had less freedom of movement than the rural poor who, of necessity, went to the well, the market, the laundry spot by the river. For all Chinese women, betrothal tended to mean seclusion or restriction, in good measure because Confucianism demanded premarital chastity and marital fidelity for females, in order to insure family stability and the orderly continuance of the lineage, which, in turn, was important for ancestor veneration. In eras when Confucianism was most rigid, this led to nearly total sexual segregation—to the point of separate closets for the clothes of husband and wife! As all this suggests, marriage was almost solely for procreation—the wife was primarily a source of sons. She was not her husband's friend, confidante, or lover. These offices could be held by men or courtesans. As a result, few wives were educated. Proverbial wisdom summed it up: "Educating a daughter is like weeding someone else's field."

Within the typical family, however, a woman was as much her mother-in-law's possession as her husband's. Both could scold or beat her at will. Realizing that her husband's first loyalty would always go to his mother, a young bride quickly set herself to producing a son—her own source of future power. There was no place for her in her natal home (all land would be divided among her brothers), so she had to comply, wait, and scheme. In proverbial terms, again, her husband's family held its head up, the family of a married daughter held its head down. If a married woman died a violent death, however, this would be reversed. Her family would go into a fury, raid her husband's home, and destroy everything in sight—their honor had been violated.

Typically, then, the Chinese woman strove to bind her children, especially her sons, by a thousand emotional ties. These became her uterine oasis in the midst of strangers. Since Confucianism thought that discipline requires distance, it encouraged fathers to isolate themselves as soon as their children reached the age of six. Mothers might feign a certain distance, but actually they were assiduous in listening, counseling, and shielding from punishment (which they were not above setting up). Moreover, the diplomacy that enabled the Chinese woman to weave this uterine web began in her earliest childhood. By age four or five, she was often "mother" to a smaller sibling. If she were to enjoy any freedom, she had to learn to control her charge(s). Before they knew it, they were doing what she wanted them to do. Indeed, before she herself understood its implications, she had an estimable talent for coercion, distraction, cajolery, and evasion. Thus, her mature art of interpreting her husband's reactions to their children began when she mediated between baby brother and parents. "Mother says" and "baby wants" regularly camouflaged her own desires. Since boys seldom had this surrogate parent role, they were not as exercised in the complexities of emotional diplomacy as girls were.

In maturity, a Chinese wife who was fluent and quick-tempered could gain some leverage against her husband and mother-in-law. By calculated rages, she could play on the male superstition that it was a bad omen if man and woman quarreled. For instance, a woman who wanted to stop her husband from squandering the family income at the neighborhood gambling den had only to throw a tantrum there to make him unwelcome. In the same way, clever women would manipulate the informal support systems that grew naturally from contacts at the well or laundry spot. If a victim of a harsh mother-in-law or a cruel husband knew how to pour out her complaints, she could get the group to take her side and mount an effective campaign of public opinion. Stung by the gossip against them, the mother-in-law or husband often would mend their ways, for few things were more fearsome to them than a loss of "face."

Nonetheless, this sort of indirect, manipulative power was about all that Confucianism allowed women to accumulate, so they had an unenviable choice of self-images: servant, shrew, or manipulator. The Taoists, however, ameliorated the situation somewhat, for their understanding of nature's way was in many respects feminist. Philosophical Taoism, which we distinguish from later, more superstitious religious Taoism, was a rather poetic view of the path to individual and social peace that stressed gaining a balance of yin/yang energies through meditation and nonviolent politics. As expressed by Lao Tzu and Chuang Tzu, Taoism suggested that social order most needed individuals with intuitive knowledge of the cosmic Tao, the way of nature. Since this Tao was gentle, nonaggressive, and supple, so should Taoists be. Since it was as a Great Mother, motherly love, as Ellen Marie Chen has found, exerted considerable influence on Chinese thought.

Perhaps the most central symbol of how Lao Tzu, legendary author of the *Tao Te Ching,* wanted people to be molded by Tao is the Uncarved Block. The Uncarved Block epitomizes a person as potential, open, possessing limitless creativity, powerfully able to become. An Uncarved Block—note that the material is not specified as jade, wood, marble, gold, or iron. The emphasis is on its state—uncarved. It is whole. No instrument has formed its mass. It is not fixed, set. If it were, it would be determined forever. So, Lao Tzu says, stay rough, natural, unfinished. That way you will have no equal. You will be whole, complete, lacking nothing. As a child of nature, you will just be—and so be in the Way.

Other symbols for the power *(te)* that a Taoist gained by practicing nonviolence *(wu-wei)* included water, the valley, the infant, and the female. Though these symbols clearly had dangerous potential for stereotyping women, the fact that they represented the ways that cosmic power itself moved, overrode such potential and set a "feminine" grace and gentleness at the heart of the way things are. Further, while Chinese culture generally thought that woman's essence was yin, and subservient to the more positive yang, Taoists insisted that yin is correlative to yang and indispensible for balance and wholeness. The result was at least a partial androgynizing of both ultimate reality and human perfection. Finally, Taoists achieved one notable practical victory when they brought about the outlawing of female infanticide.

While philosophical Taoism centered on individual efforts to achieve harmonious living, religious Taoism took a magical turn and became fascinated with the quest for longevity or even physical immortality. Its foci were diet, exercise, alchemy, and sexual yoga. Thus, some Taoists were obsessed by the yin/yang balance in their food, while others tried to learn to breath "like an infant in the womb." Not a few went to the grave prematurely by drinking elixir of cinnabar (mercuric sulfide—a "potion of immortality" indeed), and many others joined the "tantric" sects in which the idea developed that if a man could gain a totally yang body, he would never die. Since such "tantrists" conceived semen to be the essence of male vitality, their sexual yoga amounted to techniques by which a man might gain a woman's vitality without losing his own through ejaculation. This he could do by bringing her repeatedly to orgasm (when her vitality was thought available for the taking) while retaining his semen and "sending it to the brain." (Alas, it actually went to the kidneys, to be urinized.) Women were to be kept ignorant of this rationale, the manuals insisted, lest they refuse to "cooperate." (Some said that women could be injured by such "depletion"; others said that while their yin supply was endless, knowledge of the male's need would give women power over him.) Eventually, under Buddhist influence, the religious Taoists formed monasteries and allowed for celibacy, which tended to mean that women and yin became less necessary.

CHINESE BUDDHISM AND MODERNITY

Buddhism was present in China by at least the first century CE, and it had a long career that mingled enthusiastic acceptance, the development of a new Chinese speculation, thorough blending with Confucianism and Taoism, and periods of fierce persecution. For the sophisticated, its main attractions were a profound metaphysics to explain the nature of reality, and refined meditation techniques for achieving individual enlightenment. Both derived from Mahayana schools, colored by Chinese belief that nature is not an illusion to escape, but a harmony with which to blend. Popularly, Buddhism tended to fuse with Taoism and folk religion, giving the common people a potpourri of festivals and fireworks, demons and exorcisms, bodhisattvas of mercy, and omnicompetent diviners.

Like philosophical Taoism, Buddhism furnished Chinese women some help against Confucian misogynism. By teaching that the buddha-nature is present in all reality, for instance, it implied that equality is more basic than social difference. To some extent, as in India, the Sangha institutionalized this equality. It would be naive to think that sex, background, or wealth played no part in monks' or nuns' relations, but the monastic code did restrict personal possessions, forbid class distinctions, and profess sexual equality. Thus, nunneries were established where women could live celibate lives centered on meditation and service to others. This was a real emancipation from slavish confinement to the roles of wife and mother, as well as many women's first chance to study.

Around the middle of the fourth century, imperial patronage of the Sangha gave a boost to nuns' social position. Emperors and empresses established nunneries that attracted talented women, no doubt in large measure because royal patronage made monastic life a calling with high status. One beneficiary of this opportunity was Miao-yin, a nun learned in both Buddhist and secular subjects, and a gifted writer. She held discussions with the royal court and the literati, and in 385 the emperor set her over a new monastery of more than three hundred nuns. She received so many gifts that her wealth became a cause of envy, while hundreds of supplicants lined up daily at her monastery gates.

Few women, of course, were as influential as Miao-yin, but many nuns did become counselors to wealthy women. Having access to the women's quarters, they dispensed medical treatments as well as religious advice. Among their other services were educating young girls and leading Buddhist prayer ceremonies. None of this set well with the Confucians, as might be imagined, and when royal favor tilted away from the Buddhists, credence started to be given to stories of nuns' sexual misconduct, baneful influence on young girls, and the like. Nonetheless, the Sangha remained an alternative to marriage, except when persecution temporarily shut it down, and it offered widows a source of religious solace and companionship. Though nuns were quite circumscribed by their rule, they quite likely had more opportunities for peer support and friendship than did their sisters in the world.

For the masses, whose lives were monotonous in good times and pitiful in bad, Buddhism was a great source of hope. By accumulating good karma, they might gain a better earthly station, or even be reborn in paradise. A fascination with religious bookkeeping thus developed. Lured by pictures of heavenly pleasures, and pushed by scenes of infernal punishment, many strove assiduously to pile up large stores of karma "points." Devotionally, the bodhisattva Kuan-yin became a personalized focus for much of this striving, and it is interesting that though originally this bodhisattva was male, China worshiped her almost entirely in her transposed, female form. In effect, Kuan-yin became the Goddess of Mercy, object of the cult of half Asia. She was most popularly pictured as having a thousand hands, each with an eye, to symbolize her unlimited, all-seeing compassion. In the monasteries, meditations developed in which monks and nuns sought to realize the Kuan-yin within them. In the palace, the royal court discussed how this enlightenment-being was the key to nirvana. Women in the villages chanted to Kuan-yin as to a sister who could understand. As late as the mid-1950s Chinese women in Singapore invoked her in their work as mediums, asking that she help them locate and enter the souls of the deceased.

In summary, the basic religious attitude in traditional China (the overall result of Confucianism, Taoism, and Buddhism) was misogynistic—women are inferior—but the practice or treatment varied. For instance, in some eras widows could remarry, while in others this was forbidden. Similarly, puritanism waxed and waned, being softer when Buddhism or Taoism was ascendant, harsher when Confucianism rode high. Overall, however, Confucian ethics slowly hardened social norms, forcing women into greater seclusion, codifying proper relations between husband and wife, and effectively stamping out spontaneity in sexual interaction. To epitomize: even if a husband felt great attraction to his bride, he would think twice about showing it. Custom tended to shout "shame" at a couple seen talking intimately, and families were not above keeping a string on which to make a knot for each time young spouses were seen together alone. Later the cord would be exhibited publicly, to provoke ridicule at the love-birds. Footbinding, the quintessence of the Confucian attitude toward women, appears to have been introduced around the tenth century. It lasted until the middle of the twentieth century. Traditional religious honor for a Chinese woman, thus, flowed from accepting bondage. If she were a sacrificing wife, a fertile mother of sons, she might in older age come into some power over her children and daughters-in-law and merit filial piety. At her death, there would be a measure of mourning, but not as much as for a father's death.

From the last decade of the nineteenth century an elite coalition of women—mostly urban intellectuals, artists, writers, and students—began to agitate for change. They attacked footbinding, concubinage, infanticide, and the sale of girl children. More positively, they established schools for girls, newspapers, and some possibilities for a professional career. When the Dynasty fell and the Republic arose in 1912, at least a small core of women were cresting the changes. And though these more prominent women were an elite, they had cousins in the outback, so many of their aspirations soon became common property. For instance, in rural Canton from the early nineteenth century to the early twentieth century, significant numbers of women either refused to marry or, if married, refused to consummate their unions. Those married accomplished this by extending the traditional post-ceremony visit to their natal homes for years. Some did eventually rejoin their husbands, but others stayed away until they reached menopause. Those who refused to marry often took vows of celibacy and formed sisterhoods, frequently in the name of Kuan-yin, whom they believed to have been a princess turned nun, against her parents' objections. This was a powerful model; Kuan-yin had no husband to claim her, no mother-in-law to control her, no children to impede her.

This movement in Canton was not widespread, but it raised

fierce opposition, for it cut to the marrow of the Confucian expectation that women would be passive wives and mothers. Nonetheless, these women persisted for close to a century, taking advantage of an interesting set of economic and religious conditions to gain an impressive degree of independence. Economically, the Cantonese area was dominated by sericulture ("silk-production"), an occupation that traditionally employed large numbers of women. Unmarried women were preferred, for they were thought to be more dependable (no children to impede them), and less ritually unclean (not polluted by pregnancy and childbirth, and so less dangerous to the silk worms). Significantly, women's feet were not bound in this area, and female infanticide was rare, because women were needed for production, if not valued in themselves. With the introduction of steam-driven machinery about the middle of the nineteenth century, the need for men in sericulture practically vanished. Hence village populations began to consist mostly of women and children, as the men emigrated in search of work. Single women especially were in demand, so they could earn enough money to support their parents and siblings, thereby undercutting a major objection to their spinsterhood. Though the separated wife had more burdens, for often she had to support her in-laws, husband, children, and her husband's concubine (and her children), she too had greater independence than the normal, nonworking wife. Women continued at this hard work until the collapse of the industry in 1935, and as late as the 1950s, emigrees from Canton were preserving their life-style and sisterhoods in Singapore.

Religiously, resistance to marriage was buoyed by syncretistic sects that had been driven from urban areas by the Confucian authorities. They worshiped a mother goddess, stressed sexual equality, and emphasized that one was not compelled to marry. Blending Buddhist respect for celibacy with native notions of taboo, they often discouraged women from childbirth. In some areas celibate sisterhoods offered women more physical freedom than the Buddhist nunnery, as well as the chance to become an "ancestor" within a religious "family." Many girls were taught to read, which gave them access to the sects' tracts and literature that encouraged them away from traditional subjugation.

The taboos surrounding childbearing in China go back to archaic times, and have analogues with what we have seen for Eskimo and Amerindian women, but they have persisted well into the modern era. Research conducted in Taiwan in 1972 showed that either sex was still thought barred from worship if it came in contact with menstrual blood. Such blood, like postpartum discharge, is a sign of a potent female energy, and in Chinese folk-biology is regarded as the source of an embryo's flesh and bones. It is therefore both unclean and powerful, which is quite likely why it has been used by Taoist priests in exorcism rites. Correlatively, women's regular impurity has in folk religion made them fit to worship mainly "low goddesses" and ghosts, "the dirtiest of supernatural beings." The higher gods, on the other hand, are the ones honored in village festivals, organized by males. The males therefore receive the lion's share of the village's notice, admiration, and gratitude, which is a big prop to their political power.

Somewhat relatedly, this fixation with menstrual blood plays a role in the marked ambivalence surrounding females' sexual power generally. On the one hand a bride brings to a man the "power" without which he cannot have male heirs. Thus, she is a very valuable "good." On the other hand, this power is tabooed and no doubt will extend itself to form a uterine family in which his heirs are more closely bound to their mother than to himself. This obviously threatens his power and makes his bride a potential "bad." Similarly, the same blood that creates the fetus and gives life is involved in the dangers and pollutions of childbirth. It can threaten death, as well, since sorcerers employ it in their black magic. Overall, then, the blood and the sex that issues it are highly ambiguous in the eyes of folk Chinese males. Women past menopause are somewhat less ambiguous, but their long experience at uterine politics has made them masters of emotional manipulations and inducing loss of face, so they too are no unmixed blessing.

Throughout the strong folk, or traditional, or archaic strain in even contemporary Chinese life, then, pollution and danger cloud women's social personas. Birth itself is polluting and dangerous; a woman is held unclean after each childbirth (forty days in the case of a girl, thirty days in the case of a boy); mothers will be punished after death for having produced pollution. In one popular fantasy, they will writhe in agony, having menstrual blood as their only drink and clots as their only food. Only the sacrifices of being a "good" mother can balance this grim fate, and since a "good" mother is primarily one who gives birth to many sons and works herself to the bone for them, Chinese folk-women are practically doomed to internalize a very ambivalent self-image.

Reform movements, such as those associated with the New Thought and May Fourth groups (1916-1920), tried to change laws and institutions concerning women, but most of rural China continued to imbibe the proverbial wisdom that "noodles are not rice and women are not human beings." When Mao Tse-tung and the Communists came to power in 1949, they gave "the women's question" high priority. The Marriage Law of May 1, 1950, gutted the old Confucian-based system, abolishing bigamy, concubinage, child betrothal, dowries, and interference with the remarriage of widows. It stood behind the free choice of marital partners, monogamy, equal divorce rights for both sexes, and equal rights to child custody. To the party's bafflement, female protest was vehement and the suicide rates soared. Young women largely lacked the courage to face down parents who, new law or no, expected to continue arranging their marriages; older women panicked at raising children to be independent, and thus not bound to them by uterine loyalty. Marriage reform, the party gradually realized, would be a long-term task.

Contrariwise, the party's efforts at land reform found enthusiastic support among women. In traditional China, no woman could own land. The Agrarian Reform Law of 1952, which gave every poor peasant, regardless of sex, a plot of land, was therefore revolutionary indeed. No longer was the birth of a daughter bad luck. No longer could a daughter-in-law be equated with a work-horse. Each woman had in her own name a certificate of land ownership. This was a major reason that women rallied to the new regime. Moreover, their political skills, sharpened through years of uterine machinations, won women leadership roles in many village cells, and women's groups formed to alert authorities whenever old male dominance threatened to reassert itself.

For all that, the movement of feminist reform has been mixedly successful, as party reports and directives fairly dispassionately reveal. A report on "Equal Work, Equal Pay," dated May 25, 1964, notes that the feudal mentality of some cadre leaders makes them routinely give men more work-points per day than they give women, which lowers both women's morale and their paychecks. On the other hand, the directives abound in information about paid maternity leaves, day-care centers, the benefits of contraception, the need for greater care in assigning work to nursing mothers, care for older women who hesitate to mention their infirmities, and the fact that women's self-confidence had been destroyed by the old order.

The results, then, are a partial progress. Well into the 1970s, marriages were largely patrilocal, which means that women members of work teams tend not to receive special training (for they will soon be moving to weed another's field). Because married women must come into a new locale and work team, if their husbands are from another area, they tend not to gain many positions of influence or seniority. The party, understandably, has not been able to remove all stereotypes and prejudice, so there is still influence in slogans such as "militant women aren't virtuous and virtuous women aren't militant," or profiles in which women show a sense of "reliance on others, susceptibility to sentiment, vagueness in political conceptions." Though both spouses usually work outside the home, women complain that their husbands refuse to share in the housework, while tensions exist between urban and rural women's groups over the pace of change, and between younger and older women, who have been losing their power over their daughters-in-law. To an outsider, finally, there is the basic question whether, freed from what Mao called her four ropes (feudal oppression, clan oppression, religious oppression, male oppression) the Chinese woman now will have to live in bondage to the thought-controls of totalitarian ideology.

The origins of both the Japanese people and their indigenous religion are obscure. *Shinto,* the "way of the kami," was the name given this indigenous religion after 552 CE, in order to distinguish it from the "way" of the newly arrived Buddhists. In brief, Shinto is based on feelings of awe that the Japanese experienced when they were in the presence of anything unusual, inspiringly beautiful, or frightening. The result was a profusion of *kami,* awe-ful presences in strange stones, mountainous caves, rulers, high trees, etc. As we shall see, women, who could also be kami, were frequently the kamis' contacts. These women (shamanesses) color Japanese history from its earliest stages down to the present. Shinto developed into such an amalgam of nature worship, fertility rites, ancestor veneration, purification rites, divination, and so on—all centering on contacting the kami—that the shamanesses *(miko)* had quite varied careers.

During Neolithic times (4000 BCE or earlier), archaeologists suggest the Japanese venerated fertility, for they made many figurines of pregnant women. These have swollen breasts, extended abdomens, and strange, ghostlike heads. Since they are called *yamagata* ("mountainlike") they may be linked with the folk belief still influential today, that mountains function in human birth or rebirth. Ancient folktales, for instance, tell of a divine mother of the mountain who guides travelers, presides over house or temple building, assists and tests hunters. Disguised as a poor maiden with a newborn baby, one legend has it, she appeared to two hunter brothers. The older brother rejected her plea for food, because he feared pollution from the impurity of blood. The younger brother gave her his lunch and was abundantly rewarded.

The early religious complex, then, probably blended elements of Great Goddess veneration, concern for fertility, animism, and taboos, such as fear of blood. The Goddess appears related to a marked concern for securing easy childbirth, as well as to a strong affinity for maternal care generally. Centuries later, when Shinto and Buddhism had commingled, monastic ascetics would undergo rather shamanistic trials in the mountains, culminating in a ceremonial entering of the Great Womb. This was a hall hung with red and white cloths, which represented the Great Mother's blood vessels. The ritual ended with the initiate running wildly down the mountain, emitting loud cries which were as infants' first screams of new life.

Further, there is considerable evidence that early Japan was politically a matriarchy. Chinese traders visiting Japan around 200 CE found that a number of the clan-states were ruled by women. They were referred to as priestesses or sorceresses—persons of shamanistic power especially needed in times of crisis. Queen Pimiko (or Himiko), one of the best known, unified and ruled over more than thirty states from 180 to 248. Accounts of her sixty-eight-year reign note that she shut herself up in the castle with a thousand female attendants, allowing only one man to serve her and transmit her words to the people. Her remoteness and power to bewitch the people seem to be characteristics that many of the shamaness-queens cultivated. In fact, it was usually a time of chaos (epidemic or war) that catapulted such queens to power.

The aunt of an early emperor, for instance, gained great influence because she was possessed by a kami who revealed the cause of the epidemic that was killing half the population. She prophesied an uprising, as well, by interpreting the strange songs of a female ecstatic. The legends about her culminate in the somewhat archetypal story of the curious wife and her divine spouse. Ordinarily her spouse (kami) would only visit at night, but one time she persuaded him to stay until dawn, so that she might finally see him. When she discovered that he was a small golden snake, she was filled with remorse, stabbed herself in the pudenda with a chopstick, and died. He slunk back to his mountain throne, accusing her of having shamed him by her lack of restraint. Other queens, such as Empress Jingu, whose reign was a turning point in the economic and cultural development of ancient Japan, were more than curious ecstatics (or grist for a Freudian mill). They were strong and effective, if undeniably charismatic; rulers and some Shinto priests to this day count them among their semidivine ancestors.

The early shamanesses played an important cultural role, too, because, like women still found in remote villages today, they expressed their seizures by the kami in poetry. Many of the early Japanese poems were written by women, and their quality suggests that these women must have been well educated. Also, the themes of this poetry—lamenting the death of a brother or husband, praising the beauty of nature, or the ecstasy of love—suggest that the authors had a good range of human experience on which to draw. This changed, following the first serious contacts with China, for the Japanese were so impressed by Chinese culture that they took to Confucian ethics wholeheartedly. This, in turn, led to a depreciation of women, and by the second half of the eighth century, it was thought unseemly for women to rule. From that time, only severe crises opened political influence to women for brief periods, and by the fifteenth century women had largely lost all their civil rights.

Much of this change in women's status is reflected in literature depicting two medieval views—that of the court lady, and that of the ideal female *samurai* ("warrior-knight"). Court ladies of the Heian era, Japan's golden age, epitomized elegance and romance. In addition, many of them were gifted writers, for the sophisticated literature of this period (tenth and eleventh centuries) was almost entirely the work of women. The reason for this, ironically, is that men largely limited themselves to clumsy imitations of Chinese models (women were thought incapable of mastering Chinese). From the court ladies' voluminous diaries there emerges a picture of the aristocratic beauty—face powdered white, thick artificial eyebrows painted high on her forehead, teeth blackened, and thick glossy black hair reaching to the floor. Supposedly, court women were kept in seclusion, but the diaries are replete with intrigue and nighttime trysts. In *The Tale of Genji* by Lady Murasaki, which may be the world's first novel, the picture is much the same—ladies were at the center of the mannered, erotic court life.

There is more complexity in the upper-class woman of classical times than we may have indicated so far, however, because her wine parties, poetry readings, and seemingly endless round of flirtations are offset, or perhaps framed in quite a different context, by the insights the diaries afford into the transitoriness of life. No doubt Buddhist teachings had left a mark there, but, whatever the source, it is clear that many of the court ladies knew that their *dolce vita* had more than a few hollow spots.

Upper-class life, then, tended to push Japanese women to channel their creative energies into art. Cut off from political power, and too leisured to find motherhood all-absorbing, they contributed strongly to Japanese aesthetics. It is perhaps strange that the official histories of the Japanese line (chronicles assembling the traditional mythology, in order to enhance the ruling family and prove that Japanese culture was as venerable as Chinese) should have given women stronger, or at least more political, role models. Written in the early eighth century, these accounts begin with creation myths in which a divine primal couple give birth to the Japanese islands, and to Amaterasu, the Sun Goddess. She, in turn, becomes the divine ancestress of the imperial family, which makes Japan singular, if not unique—a land thinking itself directly descended from a Goddess. The early queens clearly reflected Amaterasu's aura, and the Shinto emblems of royal power related later kings to her patronage. It is true that the myths display seeds of later sexism (when the first couple produces a defective offspring, it is because she violated proper protocol: "It is not proper for the woman to speak first"), but they more powerfully reveal that women's circumscription in classical times was a fall from their early proximity to divinity and power.

By the twelfth century, the Heian golden age had degenerated into internecine warfare, giving prominence to local lords and the samurai who lived and died for those lords' glory. For close to seven hundred years, such militaristic feudalism dominated Japanese culture. The samurai mentality was fertile soil for Confucian obsession with hierarchy, rank, and protocol, and from this interaction there evolved the unwritten code known as *Bushido* ["the way of the warrior"]. Significantly, the Japanese liege-warriors who followed bushido did not, like their medieval European counterparts, link chivalry with an ideal glorification of women, often quite unpracticed. The samurai were too single-minded for that, tunneling in at terrorizing the enemy with shouts of their own exploits and those of their famous ancestors. In addition, the samurai were annealed to absolute loyalty to their lords and brother warriors, which rendered them largely unable to relate to women.

The curious result was that the bushido ideal for women made them a blend of amazon and domestic slave. First, they were urged to overcome female frailty and match males' fortitude. Many young girls were trained to repress their emotions and steel themselves for the possibility of using the dagger each was given when she acceded to womanhood. The occasions for such suicide seem to have abounded. Chief among them were threats to chastity. Indeed, the manuals dryly discourse on teaching girls the proper point at the throat for inserting the sword, and then on how, after insertion, to tie one's lower limbs together so as to be modest even in death. Another occasion for suicide was finding that a samurai warrior's love for her was threatening his loyalty to his lord. In one cautionary tale, the young maiden disfigures herself (an intermediate step, we might say), so as to bring her young man to his senses. In another, a young wife, having heard that affection for their spouses had kept some warriors from fighting unto death, wrote to her husband that she was freeing him to give his all for his lord in an upcoming battle, by killing herself right now. A third story indicates another occasion when honor might demand suicide by samurai women. Compromised by a powerful noble, one Lady Kesa promised to submit to his advances if he killed her samurai husband. He agreed, and she told him to steal into her bedchamber and kill the sleeper who had wet hair. Then she made sure that her husband drank enough to sleep soundly, washed her hair, and lay calmly awaiting her fate.

Second, the bushido woman's fortitude largely went into

serving her lord. She annihilated herself for her husband, as he annihilated himself for his lord. On the battlefield women were worthless, but in the home their martial discipline was glorious. Lady Kumano, for instance, left alone with two young sons while her husband was away at war, went to the extreme of killing them (after due explanation) in order to preserve the household from the stain of her being violated by the approaching enemy. The sons understood, said goodbye to their absent father and deceased ancestors, and were dispatched by her motherly sword. Then, assisted by a faithful retainer, she herself fell upon the suicide sword.

Bushido stoicism has shaped the Japanese well into the twentieth century, being a part of the explanation of kami–kaze ("gods' wind") pilots in World War II. Suicides by such prominent writers as Kawabate and Mishima also depend on a bushido background for their explanation. While Confucianism underlay bushido ideals, Zen Buddhism often furnished the self-control to live them out. Zen masters, from the thirteenth century on, taught Japanese that enlightenment comes through zazen, the meditation or mind-body discipline that brings a person into total oneness. As this discipline and oneness influenced the tea ceremony and flower arrangement, so too it influenced the martial arts. Understandably, discipline for women related them more to aesthetics than to warfare, but behind the selfless, effaced Japanese wife and mother of even the present, lies the code and religious philosophy that also gave rise to swordsmanship and archery.

WOMEN IN MODERN JAPAN

By the end of the nineteenth century, the samurai had clearly yielded influence to the merchants, and Japan was on the road to economic modernization. Contacts with the West increased, as the isolationism of the Tokugawa era waned, and many young men went abroad to study. Patterning with the economic role that has dominated most modern Japanese men, who have largely shifted their allegiance to business, is the female role of the geisha—the woman dedicated to this new lord's pleasure. A geisha, far from being a simple prostitute, is often an accomplished entertainer and hostess. She may study for years at music, poetry, and etiquette. Though some geishas provide sexual favors, the central part of their trade is to comfort, amuse, and relax their clients. At home, a man sees his woman as something functional: mother of his children, manager of his household, an appliance necessary for a normal family life. In the quarters where the geishas entertain, woman becomes the sympathetic listener, the ego-prop, the graceful amuser, distracter, adornment.

The beginnings of this schism in woman's image are clear in Tokugawa literature, where a favorite dramatic theme was the clash between duty and feelings—wife and geisha. On stage, the Tokugawa solution was always the double suicide of the star-crossed lovers—the maintenance of duty, with a concession to its costs. In present day Japan, the institution of the geisha is not only a potential emotional clash, but also a barrier to women's advance in the business world, because Japanese business firms still paternalistically subsidize all-male gatherings at geisha houses. This is where informal, often real, business is conducted, and where the family ties of the business group are constantly reforged—which, of course, leaves female employees out in the cold. Relatedly, large firms regularly provide paid vacations for their workers, often at the company's own villa, but make no provision for men to bring their wives and children. The Japanese business world, therefore, has little place for women except as clerks and secretaries.

During the late nineteenth and early twentieth centuries, under the Meiji dynasty, the traditional family was called the "building block of national polity." In good Confucian fashion, the ideal family maintained three generations under one roof, all solidly loyal to the emperor. Marriage existed, not for the enrichment of the spouses, but to provide for the ancestral "house" or line—to make more heirs. This "house" was patrilinear (since the fifteenth century girls had been exluded from inheriting), and the hapless bride who did not conceive rather promptly could be returned home, her husband invoking the saying, "the womb is borrowed." Alternatives, if the family had wealth, were to secure a concubine or adopt a child. The ancestral houses, too, therefore, had little honor for women.

Beginning with the prewar period, industrialization brought a number of changes to Japanese society. Second and third sons (nonheirs) more regularly moved out, seeking work, and this produced more nuclear family situations, as they married and raised children away from their own parents. Most marriages were still arranged by the partners' parents (even today an estimated fifty percent are), but the partners tended to gain more say. Women began moving into the new corporations, largely as clerks and typists, from the 1920s on, and for many this meant a modest degree of financial independence. Some Confucian rigidities relaxed, and there arose the *moga* ("modern gal")—a kind of Japanese flapper who adorned the burgeoning taxi-dance halls and cafes. Most of these were closed by the militarists in the 1930s, however, for they found such behavior and freedom for women "un-Japanese."

The occupation following World War II was a great force for change in Japanese women's status, as Douglas MacArthur pushed for women's legal rights to vote, enjoy equal educational opportunities, and be full civic partners or citizens. Women returned to the business world in force, but still to jobs at the bottom rungs. In 1978, Japanese feminist leaders, who are relatively few, considered full equality a very distant dream. Though women are fifty percent of the thirty-four percent who go to a college or university, society still expects them to settle down to marriage and a family. Holding a job is therefore just a halfway house between graduation day and wedding day.

All this, of course, relates to urban women. In rural areas, the modern scenario has been quite different. By the turn of the century, most rural folk had a primary school education, and newspapers, conscription, and travel increased their sophistication considerably. Yet the "cake of custom" remained largely intact, so that their religious, social, and political traditions were not seriously threatened. This is more true than untrue, even today. For instance, anthropological studies of village life have recorded considerable ambivalence among rural girls contemplating their futures. They have more opportunities, legally, for education and careers, but family pressure to marry and take on the hard, physical work of farming is intense. Poignantly, therefore, they told researchers that their happiest days had been the "Green Spring Period," before marriage bore down on them.

Once married, rural Japanese women today are in the Confucian situation we described for China: domination by their mothers-in-law, with the additional threat that they may be shipped home if they don't quickly conceive. Girl babies, though, are welcomed—anything for fertility! Conception usually moves the father-to-be to visit the shrine of Kuan-yin and pray for an easy birth, while the mother-in-law gets out her bag of folk-medicines. The hope is for sons, and girls quickly learn that they come after their brothers. They will be fed second, bathed second, and walk to school behind the boys. This second-rate status tends to make rural girls rather cunning. Behind their shy demeanors, they become practiced at punishing boys without exposing themselves to criticism. For example, a girl might hide her brother's cap, and then solicitously help him find it. Researchers found that boys, for all their outward willfulness and arrogance, were turned into rather dependent personalities by their mothers' pampering. This is the likely basis for the tendency of Japanese males to regard their wives not as equals, but as surrogate mothers—providers of physical comfort.

Religiously, rural Japan has never lost the presence and impact of shamanesses. Working with a blend of folk beliefs, Shinto, and Buddhism, these women have continued to function as mediums and diviners—for instance, in the Buddhist exorcism rites. Traditionally, the shamanesses tended to travel in bands of five or six, walking a regular round of villages. They would tell fortunes, pray for the sick, contact the dead, purify homes, and so on. The bands no longer travel, in part because the authorities, who always resented them, and often defamed them as prostitutes, finally tended to prevail, but many remote areas still have their practicing shamaness. In the Tohoku area of Honshu, for instance, blind girls are still regularly apprenticed to shamanesses for three to five years training, to learn the arts of trance, divination, and contacting the spirit world, as well as to learn traditional ballads and folklore. After an initiatory rite which has a marked death-resurrection motif, they will graduate and begin their practice. In fact, they may even become not general practitioners, but specialists—experts at contacting the newly dead, and thus consoling the mourning, for instance.

Over the centuries, this shamanistic tradition, which is largely a rural phenomenon now, has had great cultural impact, for the wandering bands seem to have created or developed such arts as ballad singing, poetry recitation, and even religious painting. These arts were originally for the purpose of teaching the people their folk traditions, but they have been linked to such institutions as the Kabuki theater, and the Bunraku and Joruri puppet shows. There is more than a little irony here, for classical Japanese theater barred women from the stage.

Female shamanism lingers on, if transformed, in the women who have functioned importantly in the rise of several of Japan's "new religions." These religions have blossomed since the Second World War, though they have roots in the first contacts with modernity, and they pivot on charismatic leaders with messianic claims. Usually the leaders—many of them women— have suffered great physical or emotional trauma that has been healed by a religious vision. Their new groups are organizations designed to help others share in such vision, healing, and peace. After the war, the situation was so depressed, psychologically, that millions took to the new religions' messages. Some of the prominent women have been credible holy people, a few have been social reformers, others have been charlatans, but all have owed not a little of their effectiveness to the tradition that women often have special access to the kami.

Overall and summarily, however, Japanese women have been expected not to upset male predominance. During the occupation, a man who had an assertive wife might well hear, "Poor fellow. He married a MacArthur." I do not know what the equivalent would be today, but it is clear that the shamaness' powerful, respected sister is hard to find on the streets of contemporary Tokyo.

BIBLIOGRAPHY

Beardsley, R., Hall, J., and Ward, R. *Village Japan*. University of Chicago Press, 1959.

Blacker, Carmen. "Religions of Japan," *Historia Religionum II*, Bleeker, C. Jouco, and Widengren, Geo, eds. Leiden: E. J. Brill, 1971, pp. 516-49.

Bullough, Vern L. *The Subordinate Sex*. Baltimore: Penguin Books, 1974.

Carmody, Denise Lardner. "Taoist Reflections on Feminism," *Religion in Life* (Summer 1977) pp. 234-44.

Chen, Ellen Marie. "Tao as the Great Mother and the Influence of Motherly Love in the Shaping of Chinese Philosophy," *History of Religions* (August 1974) pp. 51-64.

Cornell, J., and Smith, R. *Two Japanese Villages*. Ann Arbor: University of Michigan Press, 1956.

Croll, Elisabeth. *The Women's Movement in China*. London: Anglo-Chinese Educational Institute, 1974.

Earhart, H. Byron. *Japanese Religion: Unity and Diversity*, 2nd ed. Encino, Cal.: Dickenson Publishing Co., 1974.

Eichhorn, Werner. *Chinese Civilization: An Introduction*. New York: Praeger, 1969.

Fairbank, J., Reischauer, E., and Craig, A. *East Asia: Tradition and Transformation*. Boston: Houghton Mifflin, 1978.

Granet, Marcel. *Chinese Civilization*. New York: Barnes and Noble, 1951.

Hori, Ichiro. *Folk Religion in Japan*. University of Chicago Press, 1968.

Leonard, Jonathan. *Early Japan*. New York: Time-Life Books, 1968.

Maringer, Johannes. "Clay Figurines of the Jomon Period," *History of Religions* (November 1974) pp. 128-39.

Nakane, Chie. *Japanese Society*. Berkeley: University of California Press, 1970.

Needham, Joseph. *Science and Civilisation in China, V: Chemistry and Chemical Technology*. Cambridge University Press, 1976.

Nitobe, Inazo. Bushido: The Soul of Japan. Tokyo: Kenkyusha, 1941.

Reischauer, Edwin O. *Japan Past and Present,* 3rd ed. rev. Tokyo: Tuttle, 1964.

Saito, Socihi. *A Study of the Influence of Christianity on Japanese Culture.* Tokyo: n.d. (ca. 1931).

Smith, Arthur. *Village Life in China.* New York: Revell, 1899.

Tay, C. N. "Kuan-Yin: The Cult of Half Asia," *History of Religions* (November 1976) pp. 147-77.

Ch'u, T'ung-tsu. *Han Social Structure.* Seattle: University of Washington Press, 1972.

Wolf, Margery. "Chinese Women: Old Skills in a New Context," *Woman, Culture, and Society,* Rosaldo, M. Z., and Lamphere, L., eds. Stanford University Press, 1974, pp. 157-72.

Wolf, Margery, and Witke, Roxane, eds. *Women in Chinese Society.* Stanford University Press, 1975.

Yamaguchi, H. S. K. *We Japanese.* Miyanoshita: Hakone, 1936.

Zurcher, E. *The Buddhist Conquest of China.* Leiden: E. J. Brill, 1972.

JUDAISM

Judaism, coparent with Christianity and Greek culture of much in Western civilization, is both intriguing and frustrating for religious feminists. The Hebrew Bible, for example, praises the good wife extravagantly (Prov. 31:29), yet it also says of the contentious woman, "To restrain her is to restrain the wind or to grasp oil" (Prov. 27:16 RSV). Both balm and bilge, of course, were written by male hands in a distinctly patriarchal society. We shall trace women's image in Judaism from these patriarchal beginnings, through the Talmudic period, into modernity.

THE BIBLICAL PERIOD

As recorded in the Hebrew Bible, the religion of ancient Israel spans perhaps one thousand years (1200-200 BCE), with memories and traditions going back much farther. Developed, it is a strict monotheism, based on the notion that the sole true God has covenanted with Israel, making this people his very own. (God himself is a patriarch.) Bound together under this God, the proto-Jews made stable family life one of their strongest pillars. Quite directly, this led to a concern for controlling women's sexuality. The Great Goddess religion, for instance, which we have seen was flourishing in the ancient Near East, became anathematized, both because it challenged Israelite monotheism, and because it threatened male dominion. If women were allowed cultic prominence, and cultic sexuality were allowed religious sanction, masculine control of the priesthood and sure lines of descent and inheritance could well fall to pieces.

Therefore the prophets severely castigated Canaanite "harlotry," attempting to raze all the idols representing Baals and Astartes, the Canaanite fertility gods and goddesses.

With religious conviction, the Israelites normally married their daughters off shortly after puberty. The expectation was that the bride, but not necessarily the groom, would be a virgin, and if she was not, and her husband could prove it, she could be stoned—for betraying her father (Deut. 22:13-21). The assumption was that she had "played the harlot" under her father's nose, which was not how his property was expected to behave. Relatedly, a married woman suspected of adultery could, at her husband's request, be subjected to trial by ordeal (Num. 5:11-31). While this ordeal—drinking water prepared ceremonially—was not severe, the weight of the priestly prayers, oath-taking, and common belief that guilt would cause sterility must often have taken a high toll psychologically. At first, it appears, men who accused their wives falsely were not punished, though later they were beaten and forced to pay a fine, which went to the woman's father.

Moreover, men were not subjected to ordeal, because wives could not accuse husbands of infidelity, and prostitution was indulged, though prostitutes were maligned. Generally, then, early Israelite morality shows a double standard, women being held to much stricter chastity than men. Perhaps for this reason, if a man violated an unmarried girl, he was only obliged to marry her, after obtaining her father's consent and paying a bride-price. As punishment, he could not divorce her (Deut. 22:28, 29). Adultery, however, could mean death for both guilty parties (Lev. 20:10), because the adulterer violated another man's property, and the adulteress violated her husband's authority.

Women belonged to their fathers or husbands. On the other hand, they were not mere property, as slaves were, and custom gave them certain protective rights. For example, though women could not initiate divorce proceedings, neither could they be divorced without substantial reason or a formal decree (Deut. 24:1-4). A woman whose father was wealthy, or who was herself especially intelligent or strong-willed, usually fared quite well because Israelite society respected wealth, wit, and will. Finally, husbands were enjoined to love their wives, and scripture (Gen. 2:24) spoke of the marital bond as stronger than that between parent and child; spouses become "one flesh." Because of this, marriage became a prime symbol for God's covenant with the whole people of Israel.

A major directive symbolism for the sexes' relations occurs in the Genesis accounts of how woman and man were created and first behaved. Both accounts make the same claims: 1) man and woman have been willed into being by the direct action of God as the high point of creation; 2) they complement one another and *together* constitute humankind. This is all put dramatically by having woman created from man's rib and so to be a helper fit for him. Written from a male viewpoint, it makes primal man in effect say, "She is just what I need, an identical match for me, bone of my bone." In creation, then, Genesis intuits a basic equality for the sexes.

Further, dealing with the Fall (the divided human condition), Genesis depicts the sexes as types of early Israelite male and female behavior. So Eve, intelligent and practical, decides that the fruit is good to eat, delightful to behold, and a possible source of wisdom—a bargain. Adam simply eats what his wife has prepared. Both sin, both are punished. "Thenceforth," men have to sweat laboriously, women have to bear children in pain. Later biblical tradition (Eccles. 25:24) misogynistically makes Eve the cause of sin, but the original story simply relates both sexes to the mystery of a life that is much less than our intuition says it should be.

The other women of the Bible support this Genesis interpretation of Eve, proto-woman, as intelligent and decent. Bathsheba is a clever woman, as is the woman from Tekoa, whom Samuel used to reunite David and Absalom (I Kings 1:11-31; II Sam. 14:1-20). Deborah is a mighty prophetess, Ruth is a noble daugher-in-law, Esther was able to save her people. Proverbs 31, cited earlier, shows the sort of model laid before Israelite women, and it suggests that all woman's fruitfulness, not just her sexuality, was prized, if only because husbands wanted the richest possible production from this most equal and intimate of their belongings. On the other hand, when the Proverbial description says of the ideal wife, "She does him good, and not harm, all the days of her life" (Prov. 31:12 RSV), it may well echo a fear that Israelite men harbored. Strong women might become like Delilah, who used her intelligence, beauty, and intimacy to bring Samson low (Judg. 16:4-21). Delilah was a foreigner, but so was every new bride, since she left her father's household and joined her husband's. Doubly feared, then, was the alluring non-Israelite woman, for she might beguile a man into losing not only his authority, but his faith (I Kings 11:1-8; Judg. 3:5, 6). As the wives of Solomon turned his head, or Jezebel corrupted Ahab, so women linked to fertility gods could be trouble compounded.

The main way that Israelite women did their husbands "good" was in bearing children. To be barren was pitiable—a sign of God's judgment. If she did not soon become a mother, an Israelite wife wondered whether she had sinned before the Lord. Her troubles were multiplied if her husband's concubine proved fruitful, for often this lesser mate gained greater favor and real status by giving the husband what he most desired. The childless widow was almost a stock figure of sorrow and poverty, because she had no one close to care for her. While many of the biblical stories about the patriarchal period make barrenness an occasion for showing God's power and loving providence, they show obliquely also how dominated by their wombs Israelite women were (Gen. 16:2-4; 30:15-26). Finally, although patriarchal polygamy slowly yielded to monogamy, this meant only more trouble for the childless woman, since barrenness then became legitimate grounds for divorce (Deut. 24:1-4).

Concerning sexual love, the main biblical view is that, within marriage, it is right and good. The Song of Songs stands out for its praise of erotic love, painting a rather winsome picture of healthy sex. Its material is essentially secular love poetry, remarkable for the lovers' mutuality. The female, for instance, seems able to pursue the male without fear that she will be branded a harlot, while the male seems able to submit to her without fear of losing masculine status. That the biblical editors could include these materials suggests that Israelite religion has solid strata valuing sexual intercourse as not only healthy, but even a symbol of God's interactions with his people.

This is not to say that the biblical wife is primarily her husband's lover. No, her foremost duty, as mentioned, was to build up his house. It was by nurturing sons, especially, that an Israelite woman served God, husband, and nation (Prov. 31:1-9). It was as the mother that she had some say in selecting a future daughter-in-law or dedicating offspring to God's service. Inheritance rights often brought out the conjunction of a mother's interests with those of her sons, as the machinations of the Israelite queen mothers we have mentioned all show. On occasion, a queen mother might even seize political power herself, as when Ashaliah ruled for six years after the death of her son (II Kings 11:1-4).

Mother-love became a potent theme in biblical literature, and eventually even a theme of God's love for Israel. There are many stories of mothers mourning dead children (II Sam. 21:8-14; II Kings 4:18-20), and the mother who tells Solomon she would rather give up her baby completely than have it divided between herself and another claimant (I Kings 3:16-27) became a type of maternal altruism. In the case of God's love, the maternal theme is a rare break in patriarchal theology's armor. No more than a nursing mother can forget her child, Isaiah says (49:15), can God forget his people. Like a mother, he comforts them for their trials in captivity (66:13). Thus, when the tender side of the covenant relation came up, provoked by Israel's sufferings, mother-love was the analogy closest at hand.

Israelite women, then, were principally male-oriented. Religiously, however, they could be somewhat independent instruments of God, for it was possible for them to prophesy. Deborah, Huldah, and Novaliah were prophetesses (the last a false one). Unlike the priesthood, therefore, charismatic office was open to women, if God sent them his word. Women also are mentioned as professional mourners (Jer. 9:17), midwives (Gen. 35:17), temple singers (Ezra 2:65), and nurses (Ruth 4:16). Prostitution was for some women a fulltime occupation, since society tolerated it, but it had little status. Some women also were sorcerers, but this was perilous, because Deuteronomy 18:12 called it "an abomination unto the Lord." Originally, Exodus 22:18 (RSV) suggests, sorcery—magic and divination—may have been largely a female art, for the proscription of it says, "You shall not permit a sorceress to live." Along with cult prostitutes, females who worked outside the male-dominated system raised a great furor.

It is probably this furor, along with their ritual impurity, that excluded Israelite women from the priesthood. Exodus 35:22-29 shows that women were recognized as generous contributors to the tabernacle, but menstruation was thought incompatible with service at the altar for animal sacrifice. A woman was unclean during her menstrual flow and for seven days thereafter, while seminal emission made a man unclean only "until the evening" (Lev. 15:16 RSV). After childbirth, a woman was considered menstruous for seven days, and then for thirty-three days more. If the child was a female, both figures were doubled (Lev. 12:1-8). After this time of purification, she was bound to seek out a priest to make atonement for her.

Legally, women were under the same moral and dietary regulations as men (Lev. 11). Apostasy meant death for either sex, and women apparently offered guilt sacrifices. It was optional for women to participate in the three annual pilgrimages, but compulsory that they attend the seven-year assembly. A woman might take the Nazirite vow of special consecration to God—if her husband or father did not object (Num. 30:4-16). A male so consecrated was worth fifty shekels, a female thirty.

Summarily, Israelite women had status as mothers, but little religio-political office or power. At the cult, they were at best spectators. Moreover, their ritual uncleanness made them somewhat ambivalent, so that for important undertakings (for example, holy war) men were told not to go near a woman. Thus, though the Hebrew Bible does not favor celibacy, it thinks that pure religiosity, close contact with the Holy One, counsels abstinence. But this meant a psychology in which women verged on being religious impediments to the male main actors, and perhaps this psychology undergirt such early practices as allowing a man to sell his daughter into concubinage in order to repay a debt (Exod. 21:7-11). It is true that here the Bible shows concern for how the woman will be treated, but in grisly passages such as Genesis 19, where virginal daughters are offered so that Sodomites won't set their hands on male guests, it is clear that when the push came, many women were consigned to harsh treatment. The law did command honor for both father and mother, yet it kept women dependent from cradle to grave—literally so, since if a husband died, his male relatives were to take charge of his wife (Gen. 38). This was imperative, since women could not own property, and so had little chance to gain wealth. Only if a man had no sons, could his daughter inherit. In marriage, finally, Moses said of the young women, "Let them marry whom they think best; only they shall marry within the family of the tribe of their father" (Num. 36:6 RSV).

THE TALMUDIC PERIOD

The Talmud is a vast sixty-three-volume compendium of scholarly and legal opinion, folklore, philosophical and theological speculation, medical and scientfic theory, decision interpretation, anecdotes, biographies, and much more. The word itself means "the teachings," and it centers on the meaning of Torah—God's law or guidance. Talmudic scholarship, however, is for community growth, in holiness and social sensitivity, not for individual learning or "scientific" knowledge. Through centuries of diaspora life, scattered outside of Israel after the fall of the Temple in 70 CE, the rabbis who compiled and then studied Talmud met the challenges of exile, persecution, Greek culture, Christianity, and modern secularism by searching out precedents and anecdotes, and then adapting them to the new exigencies of faith. That Israelite religion became Judaism and survived down to the twentieth century is largely due to their labors.

By and large, the talmudic picture of woman is favorable—if she is a good wife and mother. In other words, the rabbis did not radically alter the biblical view. Rather, they nuanced it for new circumstances and the new center that Jewish life had in study:

"Wherewith do women acquire merit? By sending their children to learn torah in the synagogue and their husbands to study in the schools of the rabbis" (Ber.17a). Much concern, therefore, went into selecting a good wife, and not a few stories were told of good men who were corrupted by marrying wicked women, and wicked men who were transformed by marrying good women. It was widely held that "an unmarried man is not a man," living as he does "without joy, without blessing, without good" (Jeb. 62a). Relatedly, a woman is "a *golem,* a shapeless lump" until her husband transforms her into a finished vessel (Sanh. 22b). In fact, so urgent was the need for a spouse that "one may sell a scroll of the torah for the purpose of marriage" (Meg. 27a). Little wonder that the Holy One was said to have created the universe in six days and to have been busy ever since arranging marriages.

The ordinary term for marriage among the Talmudists was *Kiddushian* ("Sanctification"). The husband consecrates his wife, setting her aside as something dedicated to the sanctuary (Kid. 2b). He should honor his wife because "no blessing is experienced in his house except on her account" (B.M. 59a). Practically, "a man should spend less than his means on food and drink for himself, up to his means on his clothes, and above his means on honoring his wife and children" (Chul. 84b). It is not surprising, then, that though wives were thoroughly dependent on their husbands, they had explicit rights to conjugal satisfaction (Kid. 19b), financial support, medical care, a stipulated sum of money should the husband die or there be a divorce, and burial. Were a wife kidnapped, her husband was obliged to ransom her, even if it took all his wealth, and in case of the husband's death, a wife's daughters were supposed to be provided for financially. This latter provision was meant to balance the law that all inheritance went to sons.

A wife's obligations to her husband, in turn, were spelled out quite specifically. Primarily, she was to provide for his physical needs and enable him to study Torah. A model of wifely devotion was Rabbi Eleazear's spouse, who, when he was ill, cooked him sixty different kinds of food. Other models were drawn from wives who ingeniously managed to serve their rabbi husbands during their menstrual periods, when contact was forbidden. Sexually, the good wife knew that her availability not only afforded her husband pleasure but saved him from temptation. The talmudic view was that men are easily seduced ("a man should walk behind a lion rather than behind a woman"), so an understanding wife is a great guard for his virtue. No doubt, this is a large part of the reason for the lengthy discussions of menstrual regularity.

Besides physical services (sex and homemaking), a wife was supposed to enable her husband to study Torah. Such study was closed to women, though there were injunctions such as, "A man is obliged to have his daughter taught torah." Apparently these injunctions lost out to such strong opposing views as, "Whoever teaches his daughter torah is as though he taught her obscenity" (Sut. III, 4), and "Let the words of Torah rather be destroyed by fire than imparted to women" (Sut. 19a). Most Jewish women, therefore, were primarily taught to aid their husbands' spiritual development. So Rachel, a wealthy young woman, proposed to the future Rabbi Akiba, a poor shepherd, because she saw his intellectual gifts. For this, her family cut her off. She lived alone for twelve years while he was away studying (by her support). Her reward came when he returned with thousands of students and told them in her presence that all his knowledge, and theirs, was truly hers.

Such stories were meant both to encourage wives to selfless devotion and to warn husbands against ingratitude. Rav Rachumai, for instance, always came home on the eve of the Day of Atonement. One year, absorbed in his books, he forgot. At home, his wife began to worry, and then to cry. At the drop of her first tear, the balcony where he sat reading collapsed, and he fell to his death (Ket. 62b). In the same vein, when the son of Rabbi Judah the Prince returned from twelve years of studying, apart from his wife, he found that she had become sterile. Judah prayed, successfully, for her healing because, "If she is divorced people will say that the pious woman waited all those years in vain. If an additional wife is taken, people will say that one woman is his wife and the other is his harlot." The story manages, all in one, to glorify Judah's holiness, cast blame on the son for conjugal neglect, spotlight the centrality of fertility, disparage polygamy (which was lawful), and show the talmudic Jew's concern for public opinion.

As in the biblical period, talmudic Judaism found sterility fearsome—to be childless was to be as one dead (Gen. R 71:6). Obversely, fruitfulness was greatly celebrated: "In the hereafter women will bear children daily" (Shab. 30b). Contraception was permitted if conception was thought likely to harm the mother (Jeb.12b), but the great emphasis was that children (banim) are builders (bonim) of both family and nation (Ber. 64a). Children were regarded as priceless loans from God, all the more to be treasured because of their vulnerability to hurt and sickness. Thus, when Rabbi Meir was weeping bitterly at the death of his two young sons, his wife reminded him of his own teaching that a pledge must be returned to its owner, praying "The Lord gave and the Lord hath taken away, blessed be the name of the Lord."

Although all children were a gift or pledge from God, sons were generally received with greater joy. At times this gave rise to such sayings as "Happy is he whose children are sons and woe to him whose children are daughters" (B.B. 16b). A daughter is a "vain treasure." She costs her father sleep: in youth, lest she be seduced; in maidenhood, lest she not find a husband; in marriage, lest she prove barren; in older age, lest she practice witchcraft. Thus, the Talmud glossed Numbers 6:24, "The Lord bless thee and keep thee" by adding, "bless thee with sons, and keep thee from daughters because they need careful guarding" (Num. R 11:5).

Talmudic glosses notwithstanding, it was more likely mothers who lost sleep, perhaps over daughters but surely over sons. Stories abound that show Jewish mothers fussing over their sons: He isn't eating. He's too hot. He's too cold. The main worry, however, was for his soul, since religious education began very early at home. So Rabbi Dosa ben Harkinas' mother carried his cradle to the academy, that he might hear the sounds of Torah from infancy. So biblical heroines like Deborah and Huldah were praised in the Talmud, not so much for their prophecy, as for their having been wives and devoted mothers.

Concerning divorce, the Talmudists' religious instinct was to limit this prerogative to men, but be solicitous for women's interests and rights. "A woman may be divorced with or without her consent, but a man can only be divorced with his consent" (Jeb. 14.1). Only the adulterous woman had to be divorced, and talmudic lawyers tended to drag their feet in all other cases, so as to maximize chances for reconciliation. Further, the detailed procedures for preparing the *get,* or bill of divorce, and the necessity of paying the *kethubah,* or marriage settlement, militated against hasty divorce actions. So a man with a bad wife to whom he owed a large settlement might echo Lamentations 1:14: "The Lord hath delivered me into their hands, from whom I am not able to rise up." Women who gave scandal, however, could be divorced without receiving the kethubah, and scandal could include appearing in public with an uncovered head, being loud-mouthed, or spinning in the street (Ket. 7:6).

Reciprocally, the rabbis tried to ease the biblical injunction (Deut. 24:1) that gave only men the right to initiate divorce, recurring to the talmudic precept that "The court may bring strong pressure to bear upon the husband until he says, 'I am willing to divorce my wife' " (Arach. 5:6). The causes for favoring a woman's divorce petition included the husband's impotence, which was considered male barrenness, refusing sexual relations, and staying away from home longer than his job demanded. Scholars had the most generous "leave" allowed. Other bases for the wife's suit were her husband's having boils, goiter, or leprosy, or his being a collector of dog-dung, a coppersmith, or a tanner. In the latter cases, even a woman who knew before her marriage that her husband's occupation would cause him to smell bad could plead, "I thought I could endure it, but now I find that I cannot" (Ket. 7:10). Desertion, however, no matter how long, was not cause for divorce. Unless a woman could muster two male witnesses (women normally could be neither witnesses nor judges) to testify to her husband's death, she could not remarry. In relaxed interpretation, however, one witness, and that even a woman, could suffice.

Religiously, the central talmudic view that women were not obliged to learn Torah effectively kept them from full participation. Women were not held to positive commandments that entailed actions at specific times (for example, prayer), because these could conflict with their household duties. Some rabbis, though, interpreted this exemption in terms of the biblical "he shall rule over her," arguing that specific religious obligations would remove a woman from her husband's direct control. Women could not be counted in a *minyan,* the quorum necessary for a prayer service, nor could they preside at a prayer service. Though there seems to have been no law against women being called to read Torah, this was not done because of "the dignity of the congregation" (Meg. 23a). One may infer, then, that even minimal erudition in women was likely to raise men's hackles. In the same vein, the Talmud says, "Cursed be the man who lets his wife recite the blessing for him Friday night" (Ber. 20b).

Exceptions to the above show that women nonetheless came into some small participation in ritual and ceremony. For instance, they were obliged to recite the prayers that welcomed the Sabbath, and bid it farewell, to attend a seder meal on Passover, and to hear the Purim reading of the book of Esther. As well, it evolved that women were required to visit the *mikvah,* or ritual bath, seven days after menstruation, to separate the dough to make the Sabbath loaves, and to light the Sabbath candles. The obligation to visit the mikvah was but one of the laws of family purity. The other laws included those for diet *(kosher),* and since women were responsible for preparing the food, they often became quite expert in the laws for keeping kosher. Women's domain overall, however, was the material arena of home and family. The spiritual domain of public religion was thoroughly male. This meant that women were spectators at public ceremonies, separated from the men, prayed silently, and were "enablers" of men's learning and piety.

In the more general aspects of "image," the Talmudists' verdict on women runs quite a gamut. On one end there is hyperbolic praise. For instance, when the people asked Rabbi Abba Hilkia to pray for rain, he took his wife and went upstairs. Each stood in a separate corner, begging God for mercy. The first cloud to appear came from the direction of his wife's corner

(Ta'Anit 23a,b). Similarly, women were regarded as more compassionate to the poor. When Mar Ukba and his wife were in great physical danger, she confided to him that no harm would befall them, because of her many kindnesses to the poor (Ket. 67b). The Talmud also does not mind crediting women with cleverness. One man about to divorce his barren wife told her to take with her to her father's home any object she desired. When he awoke, he found himself in her father's house. Rabbi Meir, who was wont to pray that all sinners perish, was scolded by his wife Beruriah, who reminded him that Psalm 104 asks for the disappearance of all sin, not all sinners.

Women, then, may be religiously discerning. They may also be saintly. Many rabbis opine that women fulfill the ritual laws more enthusiastically than men. They cite examples of feminine piety as well, such as that of the beautiful young girl who always prayed that she would never cause a man to lose his place in heaven (Sat. 22a). Beruriah, wife of Rabbi Meir, not only was resolute in accepting her two sons' death, but she was a brilliant student of Torah, mastering three hundred laws a day and zealous for scholarship. Once she kicked a student who was studying silently, offended at his ignorance of the biblical verse that says knowledge is retained best when all parts of the body are actively involved. Still, Beruriah had a sorry comeuppance. She scoffed at the rabbinical saying "women are lightminded" (Kid. 80b), and her husband Rabbi Meir, to test her virtue, told one of his students to try to seduce her. Eventually she yielded, and then, for her shame, committed suicide. Her disgrace was attributed by later rabbis to feminine weakness.

So one finds some counterpoint to the talmudic willingness to regard women positively. In the measure that women gain religious prominence, a certain critical, even misogynistic, tendency raises its head. Beruriah is perhaps the most egregious example, but even the prophetesses Deborah and Huldah do not escape rebuke. Deborah is criticized for being haughty and is called a hornet; Huldah is called a weasel. More predictably, perhaps, the rabbis drum out a regular theme that woman is a temptress. The female's voice, hair, and legs are especially bothersome to sages, who cite them as enticements to sexual arousal. There is a tendency to portray women as sexually ardent, even rapacious, so much so that a mythology of female spirits of seduction developed. Along this line one reads, "It is forbidden for a man to sleep alone in the house, and whoever sleeps alone in a house will be seized by Lilith" (Shab. 15*b*). Excessive conversation with a woman, even one's wife, could cause a man to lose his good memory (a must for talmudic scholarship). Indeed, if a menstruous woman passed between two scholars at the beginning of her period, she would kill one of them; at the end of her period, she would just bring them to strife. Two women sitting facing one another at a crossroads are surely engaged in witchcraft (Pes. 111*a*). In fact, "The majority of women are inclined to witchcraft" (Sanh. 67*a*).

The menstrual taboos and accusations of witchcraft, of course, reveal an archaic—one might well say primitive—strand in talmudic religion, and one can correlate it with the dybbuks and golems that populated Jewish folk religion. More "rational" were the talmudic stereotypes of women: "Four qualities are ascribed to women: they are gluttonous, eavesdroppers, lazy, and jealous" (Gen. R 58.2). Women were considered garrulous as well: "Ten measures of speech descended to the world; women took nine and men one" (Kid. 47*b*). On occasion, women are also held to crave luxury, be prone to anger, and show extreme cruelty to one another. An example of this last vice is the neighbor of a starving woman who wandered over to "see what she was cooking," but actually went to shame her for her poverty (Ta'Anit 24*b*-25*a*).

To say the least, the talmudic scholars continued the biblical ambivalence toward women. Some scholars have traced the beginnings of biblical misogynism to the influence of the priestly tradition, which started during the exile and came to dominate the postexilic period. This can be traced to, for instance, Ezekiel's and Zechariah's tendency to correlate femaleness with religious uncleanness. By the end of the postexile, the beginning of the talmudic era, woman was widely considered to be impure, subordinate, inferior. As heirs to the Pharisaic branch of the priestly tradition, the rabbis did well to pick up the early biblical symbols which used female love to symbolize God's care

(Isa. 49:15, for instance), and to have an eye for the good women of devotion and brain in their midst. On the one hand, they came to call Torah God's "daughter" and Israel's "bride." On the other hand, a woman could be described as "a pitcher full of filth with its mouth full of blood" (Shab. 152a). Talmudic-era women did sometimes fight back, however. One sprightly woman, after Rabbi Judah decided a case against her, complained that his teacher Samuel would have given her better justice. When asked, patronizingly, if she knew Samuel, she replied, "O yes. He was squat, potbellied, large-toothed." For this she was promptly excommunicated (Ned. 50b).

MODERNITY

Talmudic attitudes toward women formed most of Jewish culture through the Middle Ages. While women were usually cherished in private and treated with respect in public, their legal, religious, and social status was epitomized by the great scholar Maimonides when he lumped them into the category "women and the ignorant." However, the Jewish medieval mystical movement, called the Kabbalah, stressed that there is a female aspect to divinity (the Shekinah), and the folklore, which was influenced by this, has made such parallels as sun:moon::man:woman. Originally, both sexes were equal, as were the sun and the moon. Because of Eve's sin, the moon diminished, woman lost autonomy, and the Shekinah went into exile. When redemption comes, the Shekinah will return, and women will again be equal to men. So strong was the Kabbalists' attraction to the feminine aspect of divinity that they would praise the Shekinah by reciting Proverbs 31:10-31, the praise for a good wife. Nonetheless, Kabbalism, like Talmudic Judaism, centered on study, so women could participate in it only marginally. As well, the Kabbalistic view of human nature was that it has both female and male aspects—a sort of yin and yang. The female was considered the passive and left side, the male the active and right side. Ultimately, therefore, it was the female side that was liable to demonic influences, so many kabbalists taught that women are more cruel than men, less creative and intelligent.

Hasidism, the devotional or pietistic movement which arose in eastern Europe in the eighteenth century, on the surface would seem to have offered Jewish women a more satisfying spirituality, as bhakti ministered to Indian women's emotional needs. It featured an ardent flow of feelings, centered on love of God and joy. Hasidism did not challenge the basic verities of *shtetl* ("small village") life, however, so the three blessings that dominated late medieval and early modern Jewish life continued to be Torah, marriage, and good deeds, the latter two defining women's orbit.

Similarly, little changed for Jewish women during the nineteenth century. The Breslau Conference, called by the Reform Movement in 1846, did ask for sexual equality in all areas of religion, but it was little heeded. There was a little more scope for individual women of drive and brilliance, however, as the career of Henrietta Szold, for instance, documents. She lobbied for equality for Jewish women in the 1890s, studied at the Jewish Theological Seminary, and spent the last decades of her life in Palestine, building the remarkable health care network that became the Hadassah Medical Organization of present day Israel. Not without wit, Szold regularly referred to her male detractors as "our more awkward fellow creatures."

The large influx of Jewish immigrants to the United States before the Second World War for the most part brought shtetl values with them, while those who fled Hitler were hardly poised to question traditional ways. Only concomitant with the protest movements of the 1960s, therefore, did Jews develop a strong consciousness of sexual injustices to which their traditional ways were prone. This does not deny that since the Enlightenment, many educated Jews had found Orthodoxy objectionable. It simply underscores that the religious inferiority of Jewish women, measured in terms of institutional, official status and power, was slow to come into popular focus. Since the early 1970s, however, many Jewish feminists, women and men both, have been vocal critics of the traditional subordinationism and busy about religious reform.

The Talmud, we have seen, severely restricts women's religious roles. Insofar as the Talmud still is the essential Jewish religious authority, efforts to upgrade the status of women have to shift its import, either by reinterpretation or by new legislation. For example, if women are to observe all the commandments, become rabbis, initiate divorce proceedings, or be witnesses in religious courts, halakah ("the law") has to come out differently than it has traditionally. Because those in charge of the law tend to be quite conservative, many feminists are alienated from Orthodox Judaism and operate only in very liberal or innovative circles. In such circles, they can argue persuasively that today women do not need to be exempt from time-bound obligations, both because housework is less onerous, and because men should share what burdens remain in it. Also, they can find a receptive hearing when they argue that such exemptions, at least today, almost inevitably signal to some that their prayer is not important, their spiritual lives are inferior to men's, and the community does not need their religious resources. Women should be eligible for the minyan, they say, and should be prepared, so that they too can come forward and read Torah. Especially, those women who have no husband-proxy to pray publicly for them (single women, widows, divorcees), and so traditionally were doubly excluded, need this chance to participate.

Tied integrally to fuller ritual participation is greater opportunity for biblical and talmudic studies. Without such opportunity, neither rabbinic ordination nor legal reform will be possible. As those Jews sympathetic to feminism clearly see, only when there are female judges, are the inequities stemming from past subordinationism likely to be rectified. In the same way, only if women's scholarly voice is heard, will the mythic taboos associated with, for instance, the menstrual bath ever lift. Originally menstruation was but one source of impurity, no more invalidating than loss of semen. Historically, however, it became a cardinal focus, aggregating to itself much of the rabbis' psychic fears and misogynism. By the time the dictum "the uterus is a place of rot" (Nid. 57b) had established itself, women were already the victims of a terrible legal- and self-image. The lingering effects of such dicta are only likely to fall away if a solid percentage of the religious leaders and judges themselves menstruate.

In terms of Jewish civil law, too, women still need relief in several areas, for this is often commingled with halakah. Like the deaf-mute and the idiot, women are still "protected"—prohibited from appearing in court, for instance. They do not yet have equal inheritance, marriage, and divorce rights. The deserted wife still cannot obtain a divorce and permission to remarry, unless she can prove her husband's death. In Israel, this civil statute has resulted in the widows produced by three recent wars often being doubly afflicted. They have lost husband to combat and, because no bodies were recovered, also have lost the legal right to remarry. If men were anchored by such legislation, it is said by more than just the cynical, things would have changed long ago. That things have not changed in the civil code is for many a continuing testimony to Jewish males' chauvinism and traditional religion's misogynism.

To combat this, feminists not only have called for women's access to religious studies, they also have devised new rituals, so that the image of the Jewish woman, in both her own eyes and that of the whole community, might change from that of an underling to that of a mature and equal participant. In the traditional marriage ceremony, for instance, the bride is totally silent, which has tended to enforce an image of effacement or nonpersonhood. The new rituals try to make it clear that woman and man are strictly copersons—that humanity is, as Genesis teaches, created male and female. Similarly, rituals are being devised for the female lifecycle, so that key moments in girls' lives will be solemnized, as they have always been for boys. This means celebrating a daughter's birth with a special blessing, paralleling the gift-giving for a boy's "redemption" with one for a girl's, working out *bat-mitzvah* rituals in which girls read Torah on their coming to maturity, etc. It is simply a matter of social justice, the feminists say, and increasingly their view is gaining converts.

In Israel today, one can see the conflict of ancient traditions and new claims for social justice especially clearly. The

Declaration of Independence assures complete equality of social and political rights, without regard to religion, race, or sex. The Women's Equal Rights Law of 1951 gives married women equality in ownership of property and guardianship of children. It also makes unilateral divorce, against the wife's will, a criminal offense. The Equal Pay for Equal Work Law of 1964 applies to both private and government employment. However, many of these civil rights, especially those surrounding marriage, have been diluted or vitiated by the religious courts, which will not cede their old, talmudic ways. Because of their influence, a determined husband can still keep his wife from obtaining a divorce, no matter how impossible the relation has become for her. The orthodox are not beyond playing hard politics with such issues, either, for they defend the old religious prerogatives with appeals to "national security," arguing that religion is Israel's chief unifying force. The result is that if a woman remarries without orthodox sanction, a large percentage of the population will consider her children bastards, unable to marry legitimate offspring. In the field of labor, women are protected as "women." This means that night work and heavy labor are forbidden, and also that women have earlier retirement than men. Postnatal care and childraising almost completely devolve to women, as well, so the labor legislation, overall, has not broken with sexual stereotyping.

Finally, the vaunted equality of the *kibbutz* ("agrarian commune") has turned out in practice to be less than full. Today fewer than ten percent of the women work in the valued areas of production, and since this is tied to leadership roles and committee work, the kibbutzim are now largely run by men alone, women having become the staff of the nurseries, laundries, and kitchens. Moreover, this lower status has become self-perpetuating. In 1972, for instance, only fourteen of the two hundred twenty university students from kibbutzim were women. With such a return to segregated roles, observers record, kibbutz women have again begun to worry about their sex appeal and concern themselves with beauty aids. On the other side, industrialization and the women's movement appear to be challenging these trends, and baby production may soon become less of a national imperative. Nonetheless, for Israeli women, as for Jewish women generally, the ethnico-religious identity that they so passionately affirm or seek is still shadowed by the traditional Talmudist's daily prayer: "I thank Thee, God, for not having made me a woman."

BIBLIOGRAPHY

Bird, Phyllis. "Images of Women in the Old Testament," *Religion and Sexism,* Ruether, Rosemary R., ed. New York: Simon & Schuster, 1974, pp. 41-88.

Blumberg, Rae Lesser. "Kibbutz Women," *Women in the World,* Iglitzin, L., and Ross, R., eds. Santa Barbara: Clio Books, 1976.

Buber, Martin. *Hasidism and Modern Man.* New York: Harper Torchbooks, 1966.

Cohen, A. *Everyman's Talmud.* New York: Schocken Books, 1975.

Epstein, Isadore. *Judaism.* London: Penguin Books, 1959.

Goldenberg, Judith Plaskow. "Epilogue: The Coming of Lilith," *Religion and Sexism,* Ruether, Rosemary R., ed. New York: Simon & Schuster, 1974, pp. 341-43.

Hauptmann, Judith. "Images of Women in the Talmud," *Religion and Sexism,* Reuther, Rosemary R., ed. New York: Simon & Schuster, 1974, pp. 184-212.

Herford, R. Travers, trans. *The Ethics of the Talmud.* New York: Schocken Books, 1962.

Koltun, Elizabeth, ed. *The Jewish Woman.* New York: Schocken Books, 1976.

Lahav, Pnina. "Raising the Status of Women through Law: The Case of Israel," *Signs* (Autumn 1977), pp. 193-209.

Lipman, Eugene J., ed. *The Mishnah.* New York: W. W. Norton, 1970.

Neusner, Jacob. *The Way of Torah,* 2nd ed. Encino, Cal.: Dickenson Publishing Co., 1974.

Sandmel, Samuel. *The Enjoyment of Scripture.* New York: Oxford University Press, 1972.

Scholem, Gershom G. *Major Trends in Jewish Mysticism.* New York: Schocken Books, 1961.

Siegel, Richard, *et al. The Jewish Catalogue.* Philadelphia: The Jewish
    Publication Society, n.d.
Werblowsky, R.J. Zwi. "Judaism," *Historia Religionum II,* Bleeker, C.
    Jouco, and Widengren, Geo, eds. Leiden: E. J. Brill, 1971, pp. 1-48.
Widengren, Geo. "Israelite-Jewish Religion," *Historia Religionum I,*
    Bleeker, C. Jouco, and Widengren, Geo, eds. Leiden: E. J. Brill,
    1969, pp. 223-317.
Wigoder, Geoffrey, et. al. *Jewish Values.* Jerusalem: Keter, 1974.
Zborowski, Mark, and Herzog, Elizabeth. *Life Is with People.* New
    York: Schocken Books, 1962.

CHRISTIANITY

Ideally, this survey would begin with Jesus' own, unvarnished views about women. Unfortunately, however, all our accounts of Jesus' sayings and doings stem from memories redacted decades after his death, by followers whose interpretations were colored by their belief that he was the Christ—the long-awaited Jewish Messiah. Nonetheless, mainstream New Testament scholars believe that in the parables—metaphorical descriptions that Jesus employed, especially to teach about the kingdom of God—we have a good indication of how the historical Jesus spoke and thought.

The view of women that emerges from these and other portions of the Gospels' portrait of Jesus is quite straightforward: there is nothing in his reported words that could be labeled antifemale, misogynistic, or sexist. The parables, for instance, reflect a balance of masculine and feminine concerns or sensitivities that, even by today's tough standards, is quite remarkable. For example, if Jesus teaches how one ought to prize the kingdom of God by describing a man searching out his lost sheep (Luke 15:4), he parallels this with a woman searching out a lost coin (Luke 15:8). Similarly, just as there are parables about men questing bread at midnight, or hiding a mustard seed in a field (Luke 11:5-8; Matt. 13:31), so there are parables about women seeking justice from an unjust judge, or mixing yeast with flour (Luke 18:1-5; Matt. 13:33). The man who dispenses talents to his servants (Matt. 25:14-30) has a polar image in the ten bridesmaids who went out to meet the bridegroom (Matt. 25:1-13); the man who thought to store up grain in his barns is countered by the widow who gave her last mite to the temple treasury.

This prophetic storyteller, in other words, addressed a whole audience, with examples drawn from both sexes' experiences. Accordingly, his healing and power went out to the daughter of Jairus, as well as the centurion's servant, to Peter's mother-in-law, as well as the man born blind. The woman who had her hemorrhage cured, the Samaritan woman at the well, the woman who begged for crumbs like a dog under the table—these were all as lauded for their faith as were male recipients of salvation. When Jesus cured without concern for the hemorrhaging woman's ritual impurity, or broke the sabbath law of rest to heal a woman (Luke 13:10-13), or exorcised the evil spirit from a woman's daughter (Luke 7:2-10), he showed himself to be free of the law on women's account, as much as on men's. Since women were definitely second-class citizens in the Judaism of Jesus' time, his democracy was quite striking.

Further, Jesus had close women friends. John 11:5 says that he loved Martha and Mary, Lazarus' sisters, and the whole account of the sign (semion) that Jesus worked in raising Lazarus from the dead, shows him to have been moved as much by his sympathy for them, as by his regard for Lazarus himself. In the account where Martha complains to Jesus that Mary isn't doing her share of the housework (Luke 10:38-42), this close friendship again comes through. Moreover, though later Christian tradition made Martha and Mary into types of the active and contemplative vocations, Jesus supports Mary's right to attend to him unconcernedly, without failing to appreciate Martha's busyness about many necessary concerns. (Today one might say that Jesus should have pitched in and helped Martha with the serving, so that they all could have been contemplative together.)

Mary Magdalene is another example of the women close to Jesus. Scholars of the highly artful, symbolic Gospel of John point out that in describing himself as the Good Shepherd, Jesus says that his disciples, his "own," recognize his voice when he calls them by name. It seems doubly significant, then, that the Johannine Jesus first appears to Mary Magdalene after his resurrection, and that she recognizes him when he says, "Mary." Since Jesus' "own" are those most intimate disciples who gathered with him for the Last Supper, this Johannine episode seems to mean that women such as Mary could be as close to Jesus as those who comprised "the twelve"—the new tribes of Israel. Something of this apostolic dignity attached to Mary and her mission of proclaiming the good news of the resurrection to the disciples was appreciated by the Western church, for it recited the Creed on Mary Magdalene's feast day—an honor that the Virgin Mary was the only other woman to share.

In the fourth chapter of John's Gospel, we find another important indication of Jesus' attitude toward women. First, his speaking to the Samaritan woman at the well directly and courteously both surprises her (4:9) and amazes the disciples (4:27). Second, rabbinic teaching of Jesus' day held that Samaritan women were "menstruants from their cradle"—that is, a constant source of ritual impurity. By speaking with a female heretic, then, Jesus was doubly polluting himself. Finally, because she shows faith and honesty, Jesus makes this woman a herald of his message to her village, where many came to believe in him (4:39). Clearly, he was no respecter of conventional taboos.

Rather, Jesus treats men and women simply as individuals who need his help, or as co-workers, or friends. He offers women no separate but equal way of works; he compiles no segregating list of feminine virtues. In the face of considerable opposition, and with the consequence of provoking scandal, Jesus associated with the outcasts and marginal people of his day: the poor, sinners, tax collectors, lepers—and women. It is a mark of his radical love, and the oppression of his contemporary society, that this association made him finally Paul's "stumbling block" and "foolishness." To be "for" these outsiders, he was willing, with regret, to become the enemy of the establishment. This was almost inevitable, though: if the beatitudes (Matt. 5:1-12) designate the populace blessed by the dawning kingdom; if it is the poor and marginals who go marching in; then the rich will no more be pleased by this than camels will pass through the eye of a needle.

One way, however, in which Jesus appears to have been the victim of his times was in not including any women "powerbearers" among the twelve. It is clear that he preached to women, admitted them to discipleship, and accepted their hospitality and help. It is also clear that authority, in Jesus' view, was for service, power for leadership in ministering to others' needs. Nonetheless, no women had access to primacy, high office, or institutional leadership, and this has stamped the Christian church to this day. Those patient with history, and aware of Jewish patriarchalism, will see women's early exclusion as a matter of social conditioning. Those intent on reading history literally, or defending male prerogatives, will claim that there is something intrinsic in church power that excludes women from sharing it equally with men. In matters of marriage, divorce, and remarriage (Matt. 19:3-9; 5:31, 32; Mark 10:11, 12), Jesus applies his stringent standards to men and women evenhandedly, thereby removing many of the Jewish male's prerogatives. The disciples were astonished: "If such is the case of a man with his wife, it is not expedient to marry" (Matt. 19:10). Similarly, Jesus makes adultery not a matter of abusing another man's property, but a sin for which man and woman are equally personally responsible. One wonders, then, whether Jesus' followers were not serving themselves, as much as the master's memory, when they chose to exclude women from equal access to community leadership. If they could "innovate," under Paul's urging, to admit non-Jews on equal footing with Jews, they could have innovated to admit women on equal footing with men.

The story of what his followers made of Jesus' religion is well begun with Acts. This work records that in the beginning, there were women who opened their homes to the persecuted (12:12; 16:15), instructed newcomers in the good news (18:26), were gifted in prophecy and counted among the saints (17:4; 21:9; 9:36-42), and regularly studied the scriptures (17:11, 12). Both women and men benefited from the prophecies and miracles that Acts reports (as signs of the messianic age), and the general picture is of a small group, bonded in love and sharing all things together. At the beginning, then, there was a certain idyllic opportunity for intimate egalitarianism. What caused the Christians to forfeit this opportunity and opt for making women second-class church members?

While the causality is complex, most writers agree that the Hellenistic, and frequently Gnostic, environment, which suspected matter, the body, and women, combined with Jewish patriarchalism (and the self-advantage operative in most social bias) to make Christian men fear women and insist on their subjugation. Paul's treatment of women is a good, if hotly contested, example of the tensions between the early, developing Christian theology and its cultural milieu. In I Corinthians, chapters 11 and 14, Paul upbraids women for praying and prophesying with unveiled heads, and orders them to keep quiet in church, giving as reason for their subordinate status "as even the law [Torah] says" (RSV). Now commentators note that Corinth was notorious for Gnostic ("secret knowledge") excesses. Elated by their ecstatic experiences, men and women there were quarreling, flaunting sexual mores, and defying church authorities. A woman who came to church unveiled may well have been announcing her Gnostic affiliations. Paul's words, then, would have been disciplinary ("get back in the fold"), not dogmatic ("you cannot prophesy").

The reference to the law reflects Paul's Jewish sensibilities. In rabbinic morality, deliberate removal of one's veil was grounds for divorce—a sign of wantonness. His reference to the angels—"A woman ought to have a veil on her head, because of the angels" (11:10 RSV)—may mean either that women must be protected from the fallen angels, who in Jewish mythology could be seducers, or that the pure angels must be protected from women (the ominous temptress theme). The first point to be grasped clearly, though, is that here Paul is mainly trying to restore good decorum. He never forbids women to prophesy, nor denies that they can be as Spirit-filled as men. More disturbing is the business about men not needing to cover their heads because they are the image and glory of God, while women are the glory of men (11:7). This has been a solid plank in the platform of male supremacy through Christian history, although it is balanced by the assertion (11:11, 12) that "in the Lord" men and woman are interdependent.

In I Corinthians 14, Paul's concern is for building up the church ("edification"), so he urges that all who prophesy exercise mature judgment, charity, and orderly demeanor, keeping silent when another is speaking and praying silently when there is no one to interpret their "tongues," "for God is not a God of confusion but of peace" (14:33 RSV). On the heels of this follow the words about women keeping silent in church and saving their questions for their husbands at home. The women's questions, then, he considered counterproductive—disedifying. It is a specific analysis of a specific, Corinthian problem. When he goes on (14:35 RSV) to say, "For it is shameful for a woman to speak in church," one again hears rabbinic overtones. A woman's voice, we recall, along with her hair and legs, was disturbing to the holy sages. If this was indeed part of Paul's reaction, it says dark things about his understanding of Christian faith and purity, for it means that he thought expression of femininity somehow discordant to Christian worship.

Galatians 3:28 RSV is another Pauline text important for the New Testament view of women, for there Paul says that in Christ (the whole Christ, head and members) "there is neither Jew nor Greek, there is neither slave nor free, there is neither male nor female." Both men and women, in other words, are one in the new dispensation, equally "heirs according to the promise" (3:29). The new dispensation is the eschatological ("end-time") situation brought about by Christ's resurrection and imminent return to complete history (parousia). Precisely how it figures in Paul's sketchy ethics is difficult to say, for he was not always an apostle to logic or clarity. In I Corinthians 7:36-38, he praises celibate cohabitation, perhaps because he thought it especially appropriate to the end-time. Certainly he considered virginity a charism or gift of the Spirit, but whether this entails a disparagement of marriage is unclear. Ephesians 5 shows marriage to be a symbol of Christ's union with the church, but the Pauline authorship of this epistle is disputed. Ephesians

5:22,23 RSV, as well, has the portentous, "Wives, be subject to your husbands, as to the Lord. For the husband is the head of the wife as Christ is the head of the church, his body, and is himself its Savior."

At any rate, it is clear that "in Christ," historically, there was indeed "male" and "female," and that one cause of this was that Paul, and the other early church leaders, did not build their intuitions of a transsexual equality into women's full participation in church authority, office, and life. By the time of a pastoral epistle such as I Timothy (also traditionally ascribed to Paul, but now by scholarly consensus not from his hand), the expectation of the parousia had faded. Women, therefore, should plan on being saved through motherhood (2:15). To give the full text, women should

> adorn themselves modestly and sensibly in seemly apparel, not with braided hair or gold or pearls or costly attire but by good deeds, as befits women who profess religion. Let a woman learn in silence with all submissiveness. I permit no woman to teach or have authority over men; she is to keep silent. For Adam was formed first, then Eve; and Adam was not deceived, but the woman was deceived and became a transgressor. Yet woman will be saved through bearing children, if she continues in faith and love and holiness, with modesty. (I Tim. 2:9-15)

The great Christian theme of Eve's (woman's) responsibility for original sin began here. Finally, in the last book of the New Testament, Revelation, the theme of whore and bride (Rev. 18, 19, 22) sealed women's future destiny in Christianity in ambiguity.

PATRISTIC AND MEDIEVAL CHRISTIANITY

Gnosticism, which caused Paul so much trouble in Corinth, continued to plague the church in the age of the "Fathers" (second–fifth centuries). Its dualism (matter is evil, spirit is good) went by many names, but usually it took one of two forms—either a rigid asceticism that despised the flesh, or a libertine self-indulgence that scorned morality, and made salvation a question of privileged election. In the main, the church fathers condemned both these attitudes, teaching that all creation is essentially good and that salvation entails self-control and good deeds. They were ascetic themselves, however, because they believed that "fallen" nature qualified creation's goodness and needed corrective discipline. Unfortunately, this led them on more than a few occasions to depreciate the body, sex, and women, and so to hinder their own efforts at distancing Christianity from Gnosticism.

Concerning the feminine aspects of religion, the fathers were further inclined towards misogynism by the Gnostic trend towards incorporating a female principle within the godhead. In some Gnostic trinities, for instance, the divine persons say, "I am the Father," "I am the Mother," "I am the Son." Moreover, many Gnostic sects drew the implications of this androgynous symbolism in their organizational lives, allowing women parity in leadership roles. Tertullian, a second-century African father, castigated these Gnostic women as heretical, bold, and immodest, because they presumed to prophesy, teach, exorcise, and baptize. Unlike some of his orthodox contemporaries, however, he did not forbid deaconesses to teach, so long as they were under strict male supervision. In reply to such attacks as Tertullian's, the Gnostics argued that conversion dissolved sexuality. While their own promiscuity often gave the lie to this argument, it exerted considerable influence on Christian piety. Perpetua, for instance, a twenty-two-year-old married woman and prophetess, had a vision, before her martyrdom, in which she was stripped and became a man, without, somehow, ceasing to be a woman.

Sex, then, was for the patristic age a matter of unease. As part of creation, the body, sex, women, and marriage all had to be good. Yet, as matter of experience, sex was a powerful drive, often in conflict with the spiritual untroubledness that the early Christians associated with holiness. From the male point of view, women incited this itchy drive, so women were at least problematic, if not per se evil. The best way to defuse sex and keep women at a distance was to promote celibacy. Sexual abstinence and virginity, therefore, became touted as the higher religious way.

In fact, instances of the early glorification of celibacy and concomitant depreciation of marital intercourse fairly abound: only unmarried Christians could be baptized in the Syrian church; Origen and other early Christians drew praise for castrating themselves (they also drew condemnation); marital relations were said to lessen efficacy in prayer. Tertullian taught that a failing in chastity was worse than death. Of woman, this great rhetorician delivered himself: she is "the devil's gateway," "the first deserter of the divine law," because of whom "even the Son of God had to die" (De Cult. Fem. I:1). Grudgingly, he permitted marriage (he was himself married), but widows who remarried would "harvest fruits well fitting the last days, dripping breasts, stinking wombs, crying babies" (De Monog. 16). Clement of Alexandria, while affirming both marriage and celibacy, clearly preferred the latter. In his view, marriage was solely for procreation, procreation ought to be accomplished without feeling, married men did well to practice continence, heaven would free both men and women, whom basically he thought equal, from sexuality, and women ought to hold themselves severely to modesty in clothing and behavior (Pedag. II:10-12).

In the third century, there was a marked increase in vowed celibacy and a heavier theme that women are evil. When, under Constantine, Christianity became the established imperial religion (early fourth century), persecution declined, and the red martyrdom of blood gave way to the white martyrdom of virginity. John Chrysostom, a very influential Eastern father, urged virginity because marriage was only for procreation, the world was then (about 382) filled, and therefore marriage was solely a concession to sin. For him, a first marriage was better than visiting prostitutes, but remarriage indicated stupidity. In fact, the widow who remarried would never be happy, since men like "what nobody else has owned and used." In his early works, he blamed women for the sins of David and Solomon, and whipped himself into disgusting descriptions of the female as a storehouse of spittle and phlegm, reminiscent of Buddhist meditation masters. Fathers should keep their sons from women as from flames of fire.

In the West, Jerome heaped lavish praise on virgins, gathering them as "roses from thorns, gold from the earth, the pearl from the shell." He clearly found his own celibacy onerous, mastering Hebrew partly as a distraction and discipline. For the same reason, he advocated strict fasting and bodily discomfort, for while "God hardly delights in the rumbling of our intestines, these are necessary to preserve chastity." The Gospel parable about the yield of thirty, sixty, and one hundredfold, Jerome interpreted in terms of marriage, widowhood, and virginity, and he was not above discouraging women from the lesser yield by lurid descriptions of the pain, hard work, and intimate abuse they would suffer at a husband's side.

Augustine, the most influential of the Western fathers, is not so intemperate or mocking as Jerome, yet he is hardly a booster of women: "I know nothing which brings the manly mind down from the heights more than a woman's caresses and that joining of bodies without which one cannot have a wife" (De Nat. Boni 18). Furthermore, for Augustine, marital pleasure is always a venial sin, and if procreation is not possible, as after menopause, it is a mortal sin. Therefore a man should cherish his wife's soul, but hate her body as an enemy. Before his famous conversion, narrated in the Confessions, Augustine had lived in concubinage for many years and begotten a son. One wonders what his old "enemy" thought of this. At the least, Augustine's conversion led him to find woman no full image of God. Only joined to man, who is her head, is woman an imago Dei. Thus Eve could not be the primary agent of the Fall, and woman's function in the transmission of original sin, which Augustine located in procreation, is to prompt venereal desire.

Thomas Aquinas, not a "father" but the second greatest Western influence, worked out a thirteenth century synthesis of Augustinian views of women and Aristotelian biology. Thomas seems free of the sexual obsessions that perturbed the fathers, but he looked on the female as a misbegotten male. As such, she is naturally subject to the male, and lower than a slave, whose subjection is unnatural. Defloration corrupts the woman's body, but this is only an incubator for the sperm anyway, since the sperm contains the entire embryo *in potentia*. Contraception is sinful, consequently, because it vitiates the ends for which the sperm naturally works. Even more darkly, Thomas found women to be morally weaker and more adulterous than men. Perhaps for this reason, he accepted Augustine's notion of lawful immorality: the prostitute is like the palace sewer; take away prostitution and "you will fill it [the earth] with sodomy" (*Opus*. 16:14).

In the train of the church's promotion of celibacy, then, both marriage and women suffered much ill use. How, though, did it fare for women who took vows of virginity and entered religious life? In the first Christian century, we recall, there were deaconesses (usually widows or virgins) who performed a variety of important church functions. They tended to linger on in the Eastern church longer than in the Western, because the East became more sexually segregated and needed them for such functions as females' baptism, which was done naked by total immersion. So the Eastern deaconesses instructed female catechumens, anointed the baptized with oil, visited sick women, prepared the bodies of the dead, and conducted the physical examinations that ensued when a virgin was accused of having broken her vows.

Deaconesses dropped from the Christian scene in medieval times (eleventh century in the West, fourteenth century in the East), their symbolic place in the church's esteem having been taken long ago by consecrated virgins. From the first century, women with vows of chastity had led simple lives of church service. With the growth of monasteries, a common life, regulated by vows of poverty, chastity, and obedience, started to take form. This built on an earlier practice, which by the third century had reached the point of publicity: with her father's consent, a young woman could commit herself before the assembled church to a life of celibacy. Canon law in the eleventh century reaffirmed the necessity for the consent of one's father or husband. The barbarian invasions from the fifth century on made the group living of religious life safer, so by the early medieval period it was well established that a woman who wished to pursue religious perfection, or whose family thought her unlikely to marry well (dowry was a problem), would head for the convent. Many wealthy women took refuge in convents, and female monasteries in general were an object of charitable almsgiving. In some of the convents, a superb religious life flourished, with the divine office sung beautifully and sincerely. Other convents were little more than storage bins for surplus gentlewomen.

Two interesting examples of late medieval religious women are Juliana of Norwich and Margery Kempe. Juliana was an English anchorite—a nun who lived alone in solitude. Her *Revelations* is a fine specimen of English mysticism, significant for current day feminist theologians because they speak beautifully of God's motherhood and "our Mother Christ." Margery, who went to Juliana for advice, was cut from other cloth. She was independently wealthy, and married, but convinced of her calling to celibacy. In responding to this call, she made numerous pilgrimages to holy places and had high adventures with the ecclesiastical authorities, who regularly accused her of witchcraft. Eventually, following instructions that she supposedly received directly from Christ, Margery negotiated a settlement with her husband, who was loathe to give up his marital pleasures: she would pay his debts and give up her Friday fasts, if he would vow perpetual celibacy. Once he had agreed (accepted this black-mail?), she writes, their love deepened, bonded now in friendship rather than sexual possession.

With time, however, convent life became more circumscribed and constricted, as male authorities exercised increasingly close control. Additionally, these authorities were led to pressure nuns to forget that they were women. The ideology at work here stemmed from patristic dicta such as "virgins are men in mind, even if women in body," and medieval attitudes, such as Aquinas', that males correlate with the rational and spiritual, females with the sexual and material. When a woman took religious vows, therefore, she was thought called upon to negate her essential nature. For Aquinas, women's nature also rendered them unfit to be priests, and they might not prophesy publicly because they had no authority, might incite men to lust, and lacked wisdom. It is not surprising, therefore, that priests regularly disdained females. St. Gertrude, for instance, had her writings praised by a clerical friend as, "not feminine, that is, not contemptible."

Nonetheless, Gertrude, Mechtilde, and other medieval nuns left writings of high scholarship and sensitivity, prefiguring Teresa of Avila, the sixteenth century Spanish mystic who finally was declared a "doctor" of the church. For the most part, though, the convents were not sources of quality education, for the medieval church did not especially promote women's education. It was more a matter of being of upper social class than of being a religious, therefore, when a nun was well educated. As early as the sixth century, authorities pushed for a cloister ("separation") of all nuns so strict that they could never leave, even to go next door to church. No men but priests and repairmen could enter; no laywomen could reside there; and no child could be taught or housed there. *Aut maritus aut murus* was the slogan—either a husband or a wall. Breaking cloister could mean flogging, fasting, or excommunication. An active religious life, such as that developed for men by the Franciscans and Dominicans, was practiced by some women before the Reformation (Hospitalers, Tertiaries, and Beguines), but they were rather marginal. Dominican and Franciscan nuns, for instance, had to be cloistered. Indeed, popes from Boniface VIII (1298) to Gregory XIII (1572) insisted on full cloister. Pius V (1566) made it a matter of papal excommunication—one only he himself could lift—if a nun left her cloister without permission. Written permission was available in case of epidemics, leprosy, and fire! There were women abbesses during the middle ages, some of whom held authority over men, but this was only a slight dent in the patriarchal power structure.

No treatment of medieval Christian views of women, of course, can overlook the cult of the Virgin Mary and the persecution of witches. Mary, to begin, crystallizes the ambivalence in women's image, for she is both virgin and mother—a trick that few of her common sisters could manage. She was portrayed rather erotically as "coveted of God," and praised with images from the Song of Songs. She was also seen in folk religion as a motherly protector of sinners against Jesus' wrath. In one tale an abbess who was out of her convent for two years with her lover would pray to Mary each day for protection. Docilely, Mary covered for her in the monastery and hid her sin—until one day the abbess forgot to offer the prayer. With a contradiction of images, popular piety thought of the Virgin as both the impassible Queen of Heaven and the mother under the cross, nearly insane with grief. In medieval times she became "our Mother" (earlier theology had stressed that she was *theotokos*—the godbearer), which meant that in lay imagination, she was often fused or confused with divinity.

Overall, the veneration of Mary aimed at someone so supernal that ordinary women's image and status was little helped by it. This is all too clear in the medieval persecution of witches. Despite official condemnation of the very notion of witches in both the eighth and eleventh centuries, in 1484, Pope Innocent VIII appointed the Dominican priests Jacob Sprenger and Henry Kramer as inquisitors to lead a war against witchcraft. Their tract *Malleus Maleficarum (The Hammer Against Witches)* was published in 1486, and it is a treasury of medieval imaginings about the characteristics, habits, and techniques of the evil, sexually insatiable female given over to Satan. Social historians postulate that the cause of such deep anxiety as the inquisitors' was the upheaval going back to the thirteenth century, which had involved conflicts with several strongly Gnostic groups, and disasters, such as the Black Death. The times demanded scapegoats—marginal women and Jews proved the readiest at hand. Between the thirteenth and eighteenth centuries, hundreds of thousands, perhaps even a million, "witches" lost their lives, most of them women.

The *Malleus* is dedicated to the proposition that woman is an evil of nature, painted with fair colors. She is naturally stupid, lacking in faith, and lustful for Satanic intercourse. A witch can cause impotence by freezing or stealing male organs. The authors quote a "common report": a certain victim asked a witch to restore his lost organ. She told him to climb a tree and take one from the many she had hidden in a nest. When he tried to take "a big one," she rebuked him—it belonged to the parish priest. Less comically, the authors exercise themselves in describing how witches perform abortions in which "little by little . . . fragments of the head and feet and hands" gush out. Where did they gather all this lore? Largely from confessions extracted under torture. It is a sad commentary on the limits of the sixteenth-century Reformation that it did nothing for marginal women, who continued to be racked and burned, even in the New World.

Thus far our study of medieval Christianity has focused on the West. In the East, the development of Orthodoxy, which after 1054 separated from Rome, wrote its own variations on women under patriarchal religion. From the earliest centuries, Greek Christianity held for both consecrated celibacy and sacramental marriage. Either vocation, according to influential Father Gregory of Nyssa, can heal the sexual divisions caused by the Fall, and restore the image of God. Thus deaconesses ministered to the faithful until the fourteenth century, and the devoted wife and mother became in popular piety a type of the justified soul. In dealing with Eve, Orthodoxy mitigated somewhat the Western tendency to think of her as a debased proto-woman. The hymns of Romanos, for instance (sixth century), make Eve the "mother" of Mary, and the first to understand the meaning of the Incarnation. Orthodoxy also spoke positively of Mary Magdalene, and in its sophiology ("speculation about wisdom"—sophia), it somewhat androgynized the deity, by tending to give the Spirit womanly attributes.

Nonetheless, these positive developments did not inhibit a significant misogynism. John Chrysostom, whom we have already cast as a villain, was very influential in the East, and one finds his spirit in later Russian maxims: "It is better to suffer from fever than to be mastered by a bad wife," for instance. Widows were pressured to enter the convent, or at least to live celibate lives hidden away, devoting themselves to prayers for their husbands' salvation. Men were cautioned, though, about believing their wives' promises to take the veil and so leaving money for their support in the convent: "She, cunning woman, getting hold of her husband's possessions, like a whore remarries." As in the West, the cult of Mary did not shield ordinary women from such spleen. The Eastern bishops had pushed for the *theotokos* doctrine at the Council of Ephesus (431), and their successors taught that Mary was ever virgin—before, during, and after Jesus' birth. Many feast days celebrated events in Mary's life, and miracles (for example, a plague's abating) regularly were credited to her intercession. Though the Virgin had been assumed bodily into heaven at her death, relics of her body (hair, nail parings, and such), as well as of her clothes, were displayed in many chuches, as they were also in the West. In fact, Eastern Marian iconography became a high art form, and it was popularly thought that an icon could be so fused with Mary's holy presence as to weep or bleed when witness to suffering or blasphemy. Still, in the East, Mary remained very much a complete human being, so that Pius IX's proclamation of the Immaculate Conception (1854), which excepted Mary from original sin, was rejected.

How this concern for concrete feminine holiness squared with the Russian condoning of wife and child beating is hard to see. Husbands were cautioned not to use iron or wooden rods, and not to strike eyes, face, or chest, but they clearly had the right, even the duty, to chastise their subordinates "for the good of their souls." This was true in the West, as well. Medieval town law gave husbands the right to flog their wives, and a violent popular attitude taught that if women crossed their husbands, they might expect, quite literally, to have their faces smashed in. In neither the West nor the East, then, were the Middle Ages a time for Christian women's liberation.

THE REFORMATION AND MODERNITY

The Protestant Reformation, with its doctrines of the priesthood of the faithful and the primacy of individual conscience, might well have raised women from their lowly and threatened medieval station. Unfortunately, none of the Reformation giants seems to have perceived the sexism that biblical patriarchalism contained, so their return to the Bible did little for women's rights. Indeed, by restraining devotion to Mary and the saints, and closing the convents, the Reformation removed several of women's most helpful safety valves. This was somewhat compensated for by a new cherishing of marriage, though paradoxically, marriage was considered nonsacramental, and by moves for mass education; but in terms of sexual liberation, the Reform was not less myopic than Rome.

Specifically, Luther wrote another chapter in the now long story of Christian ambivalence toward women, for he both delighted in his wife Katy and thought of marriage as "the bandage God puts on the sore of incontinence." Women can be no priests of Christ, for they are "priests of Satan." In fact, woman's main role, in his exegesis of Genesis, is to be useful for procreation. By the Fall, Eve was made inferior to Adam, and this inferiority is symbolized when a woman assumes her husband's name and therefore comes under his control. While men are out and about the business of wars and building, wives are "like a nail driven into the wall," condemned to stay at home. It is not for them, therefore, to teach or rule. Their domain is procreation, nursing, and nurturing.

On the other hand, again, for Luther, men are dependent on women in many ways, and the Fathers' invective against women is regularly misplaced. Men and women both have need of medicine for venereal desire, so if a man is impotent, he may arrange for his wife's satisfaction through a secret "second marriage." So strong is this need for sex as medicine, he said, that celibacy is not genuine for more than one in a thousand persons, and Rome has erred grievously in its institutionalization of religious virginity. In fact, Luther found celibacy so unnatural that he agreed with some medical theoreticians of his day that it would make the body unhealthy, enervated, sweaty, and foul-smelling. For women, there is the added biblical fact that their ordinary salvation comes through childbearing: "Let them bear themselves out. This is the purpose for which they exist." Like Augustine, Luther thought that intercourse could never occur without sin, which meant that a man could hardly speak of a woman without a feeling of shame.

In contrast to this earthiness and quasi fixation (some

commentators refer to Luther's "genitalism"), Calvin spoke of sex rather primly. He credited women with purposes beyond childbearing, but this turned out to be a dubious advantage, since he meant that woman is man's inseparable companion, "to help him live more comfortably." The change brought by the Fall moved woman not from freedom to subservience, but from subservience to slavery. Insofar as it is a uniting "in one body and one soul," Christian marriage should defend women against society's enslavements. On the other hand, all Christian women, whether they be virgins, wives, or widows, belong at home, subject to male control. Finally, in Geneva, an unfaithful wife merited the death penalty.

Against Rome, Calvin pointed out the inconsistency of calling marriage a sacrament and forbidding it to priests as something incompatible with sacramental service. In his own right, though, he warned couples against making marriage a provocation to lustful overindulgence. His own ideal wife would be "modest, complaisant, unostentatious, thrifty, patient, and likely to be careful of my health." Few things, in his view, justify divorce—certainly not coarse behavior, threats, mental cruelty, or beatings, for these are less important than a husband's right to rule his wife.

The women of Geneva in the early days of Reform divided into mutually hostile groups of Protestants and Catholics. Both groups were willing to move beyond harsh words to throwing stones or dumping one another's laundry in the river. Reform women would set upon convents to preach against the evils of virginity, mariolatry, and Roman abuses of scripture. The nuns, in turn, would create a hubbub, shouting and spitting, and finally give their visitors the gate. From these and other recorded activities it emerges that Reform women were more active than many accounts have shown them to be. It also emerges that they were freed from celibacy, only to be coerced into submission, justified by the biblical patriarch's dominance over his household.

It was the sectarians, rather than the Lutherans or Calvinists, who really enhanced women's social and theological standing. For instance, both Baptists and Brownites (the ancestors of the

Congregationalists) had women preachers by the middle of the seventeenth century. George Fox, founder of the Quakers, thought Christianity aimed at restoring the sexual equality of Paradise, and the roster of Quaker saints included Margaret Fell ("nursing Mother of Quakerism"), Elizabeth Houton (preached in England, Jamaica, and the Colonies), Mary Dyer (martyred in Boston), Elizabeth Fry (prison reformer and abolitionist), and Sarah Grimke (abolitionist and feminist). Though the Puritans thought women too unclean to administer baptism, they did emphasize that marriage was for mutual companionship and love, even more than for intercourse and procreation. John Milton held that without genuine compatibility, there could be no true marriage, but the Puritans allowed only men to discern incompatibility and sue for divorce. A woman was to win love by docility.

In the nineteenth century, Mary Baker Eddy founded Christian Science and replaced the Christian God the Father with a Father-Mother deity, more potent for curing sickness. Eddy's religion called sickness and sin illusions, based on the deeper illusion that the body is real. Without a body, a woman could be man's spiritual equal. The painful biography that Eddy traveled on the way to this conclusion included escaping a stern Calvinist father and overcoming the wispy, fainting gentility that was supposed to mark a lady in her day. Her Father-Mother God owed much to Ann Lee, who in 1774 had brought the Shakers to America from England. Lee was a charismatic who focused redemption on a male-female couple—Jesus and herself. She underwent great personal suffering (poverty, an unhappy marriage, the deaths of four infants), only to emerge with great faith that salvation was available through asceticism and celibacy. Her Shaker community practiced full sexual equality and strict celibacy, based on unions with Christ similar to her own mystical marriage to him.

Utopian, visionary, ecstatic, these foundresses broke with, or reformed, Protestant Christianity within one hundred fifty years of its birth, carrying on the initiatives of women in the early Gnostic sects and such orthodox nontraditionalists as Margery Kempe. Katy Luther and Idelette Calvin, on the other hand, stayed at home, but they and other more traditional women made home a center of piety and culture. By their full share in the excitement and uncertainty of the early Reformation, they gave some added credibility to the new notion of lay dignity.

Catholic women of the Counter-Reformation included prominently the many nuns who, from the sixteenth century, strove to overcome cloister and offer themselves for works of social service. Their success was at best mixed. Angela Merici, for instance, founded the Ursulines to vitalize Christian families by teaching women and children at home. She won papal approval and the attention of Charles Borromeo, Bishop of Milan. He invited the Ursulines to work in his diocese, but then insisted that they observe full cloister. At the same time, Ursulines of a splinter group were having good success in Paris, until they incurred the annoyance of certain Jesuit priests, who saw to it they were returned to cloister. The Daughters of Charity, founded by Vincent de Paul and Louise de Marillac, learned from this pattern and never became nuns. By taking no public vows and wearing no religious habit, they remained free to nurse and serve the poor. Ironically, then, the only religious women who could do active works of mercy were those who did not profess their religious status officially. So strong were the controls of the Catholic reform initiated at the Council of Trent in the sixteenth century, that not until 1900 were nuns officially granted the right to an active life.

In recent times, Karl Barth's theology has greatly influenced Protestant churches in both Europe and America, so feminist writers regularly probe his view of women. In such a probe, Barth's biblical God turns out to be both master and masculine, a creator who has ordered the sexes in such wise that woman is definitely derivative from man. This is not to imply, he says, any impairment of woman's dignity, lessening of the sexes' need for one another, injustice, or special privilege—a trick that Barth himself may have been able to bring off, but few of his readers could manage. As his *Church Dogmatics* (3:4) puts its, woman's religious task is to obey the order inherent in nature from creation. Specifically, she is to be B to man's A—A initiates and stimulates; B follows A, complies and collaborates. If a man abuses his natural preeminence, neither is the divine order vitiated, nor is woman's revolt justified. By keeping to her own place, despite all abuse, she will be found victorious by God. Out of his own writings, contemporary women are reading Barth back, "There have always been far too many male or masculine theologians" (*C.D.* 3:4, p. 155).

Paul Tillich, the other most significant recent Protestant systematician, has a concept of God as the "Ground of Being" that many have found potentially liberating. In addition, Tillich, more than Barth, has pondered the significance of culture and made it an intrinsic partner to theological dialogue. He has written little explicitly about women or their religio-cultural conditioning, but his "Ground of Being" allows for both masculine and feminine attributes, and his analysis of human reason has an important place for affectivity. Without being disciples, recent feminist theologians such as Mary Daly have drawn on portions of Tillich's systematic thought.

Catholic women, until very recently (fifteen years ago), were struggling simply to gain breathing space. The 1912 edition of the *Catholic Encyclopedia,* for instance, claimed that women are "inferior in some respects to men both in body and in soul." It found women's struggles for equality in employment and pay "not compatible with the standard of the gospel," and said that "the sexes can never be on an equality as regards studies pursued at a university." Woman's real power lies in her "indirect influence," and this "would suffer severe injury by political equality." From all this the encyclopedia concludes that even "common sense" concurs with the Church's opposition to women's suffrage.

The 1967 edition of the *Catholic Encyclopedia* rectifies this sexism, but the 1917 Code of Canon Law, though long in process of reform, has yet to be rectified. Somewhat like the Talmud, Canon law is hard to change, because those trained in it tend to develop a mentality that makes them reluctant to let social shifts influence long-held tradition. Specifically, Canon law not only forbids the ordination of women as priests but even prohibits their serving at Mass, if a man is available. If a woman should be called on to serve Mass, she must make the prayer responses from outside the sanctuary, unlike men, who may approach the altar. Women are not to baptize unless there is an emergency, and no men are present, and it is only recently that Canon 845 has been relaxed to allow laymen or nuns but not laywomen, to distribute Communion in the absence of a priest. Women lectors (readers of scriptural passages) have also been forbidden, and the whole distancing of women from Catholic religious ceremony suggests a lingering fear of "pollution."

Perhaps the most offensive area of Canon law, however, deals with the procedures it lays down in marriage cases, specifically with the physical examinations required in instances where an annulment is being sought on grounds of nonconsummation. In 1942, an inquiry aimed at clarifying who may and should conduct this hymenal examination resulted in an instruction from the Holy Office that physicians (male doctors) are required, and any evidence given by "women with a doctor's degree" must be corroborated by a "physician." The judge in this procedure is supposed to instruct the examinee that she is to take a thirty-minute bath beforehand, and the investigators are supposed to provide detailed information about the hymen's form, type, size, position, and elasticity. Following all this, the woman, who has already suffered the trauma of marital failure and the degradations of the physical examination, can expect to be questioned by a panel of priests.

Changes are afoot among Catholic and Protestant feminists, of course, as they attack Christian misogynism across a wide front of theological, denominational, and socio-political issues. Theologically, the first objects of assault have been the scriptural and traditional teachings that have been cited historically as proofs of women's inferiority. Related to this debunking or demythologizing has been an effort to demisogynize the language, symbols, and doctrines in which the tradition has developed. More positively, feminist theologians have taken on the central task of depatriachalizing the biblical God, so that divinity may begin to appear as both female and male, as well as beyond all sexual limitations. By initiating new rituals, symbolizations, and models, the feminists also hope to restore Christian women's sense of pride and self-worth. Elisabeth

Schussler Fiorenza, for instance, has developed the image of Mary Magdalene, showing the richness she might bear for contemporary women as a paradigm for their faith.

On denominational issues, women's ordination is a rallying cry or organizing focus, for it epitomizes the injustice, if not hypocrisy, that many see in the churches' preaching of human rights, and then refusing to grant basic dignity and equal opportunity to more than half their own membership. Many Protestant denominations, of course, do ordain women, but both the Roman Catholics and Orthodox, whose combined membership is close to a billion, do not. Mere ordination, however, is not enough, as recently ordained Episcopal women have experienced. Almost all the denominations collude, semi-wittingly, in what one report calls the "trivialization" of women, thereby miserably failing their prophetic charge. It is in terms of equal access to positions of authority, pay, dignity, liturgical leadership, and outlet for their talents that those struggling to keep their feminism and their Christian faith together will judge their denominations, and at present, any denomination with courage to hear will get more than an earful.

Lastly, socio-political issues cannot be separated from theological and infradenominational ones, for Christian feminists are as sensitive as any other feminists to abortion, divorce, gay rights, the ERA and other battlegrounds. Perhaps the saddest portion of the current picture among Christian women is the way, with a good deal of manipulation from male powerholders, they have been set against one another as conservatives and liberals, evangelicals and radicals, right-to-lifers and right-to-choicers. In the Bible belt I have witnessed fundamentalist churches combining with Roman Catholics to vote down civil rights for gay people, while the whole matter of what the churches don't do regarding sex education, black people, day-care centers, concern for single women, help for battered wives and children, and so on is a serious blow to their credibility. The German philosopher Friedrich Nietzsche, who was no friend of women, cynically wrote that the last Christian died on the cross. Christian feminists want to confute Nietzsche, but they find their churches giving him a lot of help.

BIBLIOGRAPHY

Arseniev, Nicholas. *Russian Piety*. London: The Faith Press, 1964.

Bassett, William W. "Canon Law and Reform: An Agenda for a New Beginning," *Toward Vatican III*, Tracy, David, ed. New York: Seabury Press, 1978, pp. 196-213.

Cooke, Bernard. *Ministry to Word and Sacraments*. Philadelphia: Fortress Press, 1976.

Clark, Elizabeth, and Richardson, Herbert, eds. *Women and Religion: A Sourcebook of Christian Thought*. New York: Harper & Row, 1977.

Fedotov, George P. *The Russian Religious Mind*. Cambridge: Harvard University Press, 1946.

Fiorenza, Elisabeth Schussler. "Feminist Theology," *Theological Studies* (December 1975), pp. 605-26.

Gremillion, Joseph. *The Gospel of Peace and Justice: Catholic Social Teaching Since Pope John*. Maryknoll, N.Y.: Orbis Books, 1976.

Heyward, Carter, and Hiatt, Suzanne R. "The Trivialization of Women," *Christianity and Crisis* (June 26, 1978), pp. 158-62.

Hughes, Pennethorne. *Witchcraft*. Baltimore: Penguin Books, 1965.

Lossky, Vladimir. *The Mystical Theology of the Eastern Church*. Crestwood, N.Y.: St. Vladimir's Press, 1976.

McGrath, Sister Albertus Magnus, O.P. *What a Modern Catholic Believes about Women*. Chicago: Thomas More Association, 1972.

Meeks, Wayne A. "The Image of the Androgyne: Some Uses of a Symbol in Earliest Christianity," *History of Religions* (February 1974), pp. 165-208.

Ruether, Rosemary R., ed. *Religion and Sexism: Images of Women in the Jewish and Christian Traditions*. New York: Simon & Schuster, 1974.

Setta, Susan. "Denial of the Female: Affirmation of the Feminine. The Father-Mother God of Mary Baker Eddy," *Beyond Androcentrism*, Gross, Rita M., ed. Missoula: Scholars Press, 1977, pp. 289-304.

Tavard, George H. *Woman in Christian Tradition*. University of Notre Dame Press, 1973.

Warner, Marina. *Alone of All Her Sex: The Myth and Cult of the Virgin Mary*. London: Weidenfeld and Nicholson, 1976.

ISLAM

The youngest of the world religions is a strict monotheism whose basis is a series of revelations given to the prophet Muhammad in the years 611-621 CE. Since Muhammad experienced the revelations as a command to "recite," this compilation is called the *Qur'an* ("Koran"), "recitals." At the core of the Qur'an is a simple, stark confession of faith: "There is no god but Allah, and Muhammad is his prophet." The proper response to God ("Allah") is total submission, and this is what "Islam" and "Muslim" both signify. Prior to Muhammad, Muslims teach, God spoke through other prophets—Abraham, Moses, Jesus. Muhammad, however, is the definitive climax to this prophetic line, its "seal," and Islam's religious program is the consummation of revealed religion. The best epitome of how Islam works out in practice is its own summary, the five "pillars": (1) confession of central belief (noted above); (2) prayer five times each day; (3) fasting during the lunar month of Ramadan; (4) almsgiving; (5) pilgrimage to Mecca at least once during one's lifetime. What the pillars prop is remembrance *(dhikr)* of God's presence, sovereignty, judgment, and mercy.

From its beginning in the Arabian peninsula, Islam spread rapidly, and today it is a major force not only in the Middle East, but in Africa, Pakistan, Indonesia, China, and the Soviet Union. Indeed, it is the fastest growing world religion. Moreover, it has been Islam's way to influence cultures deeply, for it presents itself as a total world-view and has little patience with distinctions between the religious and the secular. In dealing with the Qur'anic view of women, women in traditional Islam, and modern Muslim views, therefore, we will be cutting close to the heart of millions of Iranian, Algerian, Turkish, Indonesian, Iraqi, and even American lives.

THE QUR'ANIC VIEW OF WOMEN

Scholarly consensus about the implications of Muhammad's revelations for women is that they were of considerable benefit, for in the period just prior to the birth of Islam, Arabian women had few rights. Ancient Arabia, however, has left some evidences that it was a matriarchy, or at least a matrilineal society. The earliest poetry portrays women as brave warriors and possessors of high social status. It is likely that polyandry ("plural husbands") was customary, with both lineage and inheritance following matrilineal descent. In the *sadiqa* marriage arrangements of that time, a woman chose her husband herself, received a gift tokening his desire, and divorced him at her pleasure. After the marriage, they lived in her tribe, to which their children were accounted. Because the sadiqa marriage was essentially a matter of mutual consent between the partners, it required neither witnesses nor guardians. At the least, then, some women in ancient Arabia had powerful claims to equality.

Alongside the sadiqa marriage, apparently, was the *ba'l* marriage, which was rigidly patriarchal. In its earliest form, this marriage was by capture. Later, women were bought, their fathers or nearest male relatives being paid a bride-gift price for the right to them and any future children. In these cases, brides went to their husbands' tribes and had no rights to divorce or inheritance. One conjecture is that the ba'l marriage originally concerned only captive or alien women. Gradually, however, it replaced the sadiqa marriage and became the norm. This was part of a general shift toward patriarchy, serving men's desires to secure a patrilineal form of inheritance and family organization. The result for women was an end to equality and a repressive stress on premarital chastity.

By Muhammad's time, ba'l marriages were the rule, and women were chattel. In fact, the nomadic tribes of seventh century Arabia were both patriarchal and polygamous, a man being entitled to as many wives as he could buy or steal. As property, women were passed from their fathers to their husbands, and then, if their husbands died, to their husbands' sons. (Islam banned marriages between stepsons and widows as "odious.") Because sons were highly prized, the birth of a daughter could be felt shameful, and female infanticide ran high. Further, women were neither hunters nor warriors, so they were economically marginal. Debilitated by frequent pregnancies and malnutrition, they were easy prey for marauders, and a source of intertribal warfare. The upshot was that women's only value was as the source of sons. As proverbial reflection put it, "A man can bear anything but the mention of his wives," or "Women are the whips of Satan," or "Trust neither a king, a horse, nor a woman."

The Qur'an, which Muhammad's followers have almost all regarded as literally the Word of God, attempted to shift allegiance from the tribe to a broader religious community. This, in turn, shifted focus from the tribal unit to the extended family. As a result, the Qur'an opposed female infanticide (Surah 16:58,59) and sought to protect women in matters of marriage, divorce, and inheritance, basing their rights on a fundamental religious equality with men, in submissive dependence on Allah. In marriage, the Qur'an required the woman's consent and made her the recipient of the bride-gift. It limited polygamy to four wives, if a man could provide for all of them and deal with them "justly" (4:3). Muhammad is thought to have preferred monogamy, but was forced to compromise with the previously unlimited polygamy, in part because incessant warfare had decimated the male population.

On divorce, the Qur'an's allowance appears reluctant, for it repeatedly urges reconciliation (2:228 ff.), demands a three-month waiting period, in part to assure that the wife is not pregnant, and provides that the husband support her during the waiting time, and to term, if she is pregnant. Women have divorce rights, too—for instance, on grounds of desertion; if a woman initiates divorce proceedings, though, her husband can keep part of her dowry. Short of divorce, the Qur'an gives a woman the right to claim damages before the judge of the religious court, if she has been abused. Finally, by limiting a husband's right to divorce the same woman repeatedly (twice became the maximum), the Qur'an somewhat hedged male caprice. Women also gained from the Qur'an's reform of patriarchal inheritance customs, becoming heirs with rights to half their brothers' portions. (Males had to provide for all their dependents.) Women could have title to their own jewelry, and also to their own earnings.

Religiously, both sexes are obligated to the five pillars and are eligible for salvation or damnation, according to their personal merits (4:124; 33:73; 6:51; 10:3). Contrary to later custom, women prayed in the mosques during Muhammad's time, and there are evidences that in the early centuries there were convents of Islamic women. Religious education was open to women, and the first centuries developed female scholars and saints. Overall, then, the Qur'an improved Arabian women's lot considerably.

So goes the majority scholarly opinion, but it is sometimes challenged by reference to the case of Khadijah, Muhammad's first wife. She was independently wealthy: a caravan owner, merchant, and widow. Were pre-Islamic women, then, as oppressed as the majority view maintains? Yes, because Khadijah only came into her wealth and independence by outliving all her male kin—by falling outside the system. For the vast majority of women, therefore, the Qur'an was, in theory, a considerable innovation and elevation, although its practical effects are debated. The rapid dissolution of Qur'anic rights after Muhammad's death renders the effectiveness of the Prophet's reforms even during his lifetime questionable, and the bottom line in the Qur'an itself is that males have power over females: "Men are in charge of women, because Allah hath made one of them to excel the other, and because they spend their property" (for women's support). Therefore, "good women are the obedient." "As for those from whom you fear rebellion, admonish them and banish them to beds apart and scourge them" (4:38). Some apologists for Islam omit this portion of the Qur'an's view of women, doing their scholarly credibility little service.

Also on the debit side, the Qur'an gives comfort to later Muslims who sought enforced veiling and *purdah* ("seclusion" or "harem"). Surah 33:59, where women are told to cover their persons when abroad to avoid insult, probably had in mind only local conditions in the Mecca of Muhammad's time, but it was later used to justify veiling. Other passages are quite explicit about the sexual danger emanating from women (a major justification for veiling). For instance, 33:53 has "And when you ask anything of them [the prophet's wives] ask it from behind a curtain. That is purer for your hearts and their hearts." In 2:282, one reads that two women equal one man as witnesses in court, while 2:223 describes women as fields for men to seed at their pleasure. The Qur'an does denounce debauchery (4:24) and shows a concern for women's sexual needs (4:129), but much in the Qur'anic image of women is negative. Menstruation, finally, caps this negative image, for the Qur'an regards it as an illness or source of uncleanness. Religious equality therefore is *only* before Allah. It does not entail social equality or opportunity for power.

THE TRADITIONAL MUSLIM VIEW OF WOMEN

There is near unanimity among scholars of Islam that the centuries following the Prophet's death brought a decline in women's status. Conservative scholars designate the period from the tenth to the fourteenth centuries as the era when Muslim women's freedom finally slipped away; others place its loss earlier. Among the causes most regularly mentioned are the misogynism of the areas outside Arabia into which Islam spread, the totally male dominance of Muslim authority, and the influence of the traditions about the Prophet *(hadith)*. In Syria, Persia, Egypt, and India, for instance, Islam moved into very patriarchal cultures. Thus, when Persian poetry later depicts women as erotic and empty-headed, this is probably due as much to pre-Islamic influence as to anything strictly Muslim. Concerning authority, it is hard to say whether male power caused female seclusion in later centuries or resulted from such seclusion (chicken or egg?). Either way, men fought the wars, administered the laws, and wrote the scholarship—while poets celebrated women as passionate toys, voluptuous manikins. Since the Qur'an entailed neither a male priestly caste nor a prohibition on women's education, the nearly complete exclusion of women from Muslim ritual or scholarship through the long traditionalist centuries seems especially tragic.

The hadith, of course, were not generated apart from this increasingly sexist society. It is not surprising, then, that they became increasingly misogynistic, reading back onto the Prophet the prejudices of later times, and thereby sanctioning them. The major collections of traditions stem from the ninth century, and they contain such unlikely stories as that: a) Muhammad, by special vision, perceived that the majority of those in the Fire (hell) are women; b) the Prophet said that were idolatry not forbidden, he would order a wife to bow down to her husband as he enters her, because it is then that God's grace is upon her; and c) Muhammad said that a woman cannot realize the intense joy of faith until she submits to her husband physically.

The upshot of these and other causal factors was that in practice, Islam soon revoked the rights granted women in the Qur'an. Closely woven into all her diminution of rights was the Muslim woman's veiling and purdah, because these removed her completely from the public realm, under threat of at least scorn and character assassination. In an increasingly puritanical or repressed atmosphere, Qur'anic rules of modesty such as 24:31 were invoked to prove that a woman's whole body is pudendal, and so deserves purdah. For men, avoidance became virtue: "Allah will reward the Muslim who, having beheld the beauties of woman, shuts his eyes." Similarly, men were not to visit absent friends' homes for "the devil circulates within you like the blood in your veins." There was even a farfetched overflow of this caution to warn women themselves: two women were not to sit together, lest one later describe the other to her husband and he be tempted.

Because of purdah, women no longer could frequent mosques, and since the mosques were cultural and educational centers, as well as religious foci, women soon became completely marginal culturally. They were shunted into the backwaters socially, psychologically, and economically which impeded their whole human development. So impeded, they were unfit for public life—a vicious circle practically impossible to stop. This was especially true of middle and upper-class women, for peasant women had to farm, cook, and weave. Their lives were hard, but some of them had a little dignity as midwives, nurses, or fortunetellers. Religiously, women's seclusion meant that they had little instruction in their faith or encouragement to fulfill its duties. Therefore, Muslim women generally became woefully superstitious or uninterested. One survey done in the 1950s opined that ninety percent of Islam's veiled women neither prayed nor performed their other obligatory religious duties.

By five centuries after the Prophet's death, then, a woman was again chattel—property of her father until purchased by a husband, whose control over her was absolute. In effect, most of women's Qur'anic rights had disappeared. They no longer had a say in their own marriages; the bride-gift went to their families; enhancing family status became their fathers' main goal in marrying them off. In a reversion to pre-Qur'anic custom, many partners were married as children, the little bride being sold on the model of the old b'al marrige. Once sold, the wife was so totally under her husband's control that she could be imprisoned for withholding obedience to him, a practice that continued in Egypt into the 1970s. Another abolition of Qur'anic legislation was the circumventing of women's rights to inherit. By a device called the *waqf* ("religious endowment"), a family would list those who were to share in its estate, leaving daughters unmentioned. Similarly, by the time Islamic tradition had crystallized, divorce had become solely a male prerogative, even the Qur'anic stipulation of a waiting or cooling-off period being disregarded. Now the husband had only to say, "I divorce you," three times, or even, "I divorce you three times." And whereas the Qur'an required four witnesses to establish a charge of adultery, the traditionalists would consider a wife guilty of this charge on the basis of her husband's swearing to it four times.

Cases of child custody were now almost automatically settled in the father's favor (there were numerous women in his extended family to care for such children), and women who did not produce a male heir would regularly be divorced, another practice that still obtains in some Muslim countries.

As some of our remarks indicate, traditional Islamic views—the interpretations that crystallized by the time Islam had spread outside Arabia and settled in other cultures—have remained in force well into the twentieth century. There are reform movements afoot now which suggest that change is accelerating, so the future may well be different. In 1972, however, a woman in Marrakech, deserted by her husband, still could epitomize the powerlessness that her Islamic sisters had suffered for well over ten centuries. This woman's family refused to support her moves for divorce from the deserter, on the grounds that he was "family" (a first cousin), and that the publication of his behavior would soil their reputation. They preferred to take her and her daughter in themselves. On her own, the woman had no possible way of prosecuting the divorce proceedings or supporting herself and her child. Though well educated, she was still legatee of the traditions, such as purdah, which kept women solely dependent on male control and support—barefoot, pregnant, and impotent, we might say. Only men had money to pay the piper, so only men called the tunes. Women at the ends of the spectrum (Bedouin laborers or indolent harem ladies, for instance) tended to prove this rule. The Bedouins were both despised and somewhat independent because they worked and were economically important. The harem ladies' indolence was thought a great tribute to their male owner's great wealth and power.

One can join this analysis of female impotence to descriptions of typical Muslim family life and write a scenario lived by perhaps eighty-five percent of Muslim women for hundreds of years. In it, the family would be agrarian, extended, basically self-sufficient, though terribly poor, and organized with a clear division of labor. A female's role was to be docile as a daughter, submissive as a wife, prolific in bearing children, strong as a mother-in-law, doting as a grandmother, supportive as an aunt.

Her key role, however, was as an "envelope for conception"—above all, the conception of sons. Indeed, most Muslim women were referred to as X, mother of Y. No wonder proverbs spoke of menopause as the age of despair. The female role, in other words, was as an instrumentality. Boys were "the tent peg of the house," good wishes came as hopes that one have "seven sons and seven pilgrimages." Because folklore said that the dominant parent determined an embryo's sex, to be the father of girls undermined a man's virility. For these and many other reasons, then, at the birth of a little girl "the threshold of a house weeps for forty days."

A revealing entry into male Muslims' perceptions of women comes from materials about the afterlife (Judgment was a major Qur'anic concern). Many hadith have Muhammad testifying to the high female population of hell—basically because so many women are ungrateful and unfaithful to their husbands. Since ingratitude and infidelity to Allah were cardinal sins for males, the striking aspect of these testimonies was that women were thought condemned, not for their failures vis-à-vis Allah, but for their failures vis-à-vis their husbands. In a religion horrified of idolatry, this indicates an extraordinary degree of blindness—or male presumption.

It is women's biological nature that does them in, according to other hadith, however, because due to menstrual weakness, they often do not fast and pray. Fasting itself was problematic for women, however, because it could make them less available to their husbands or less acrobatic. Therefore the Prophet is said to have made women's fasting contingent on their husbands' permission. According to *Ms.* magazine (5/9), as recently as 1977, a woman's failure to obtain such permission resulted in her being shot and killed. Finally, women also predominate in the Fire because they lack sufficient intelligence to be saved: "A woman is a woman and the Prophet—God's prayers and peace on him—said that women are lacking in mind and religion." All this is a far cry from the Qur'an's insistence on the *personal* responsibility for salvation or damnation.

Moreoever, those women who are saved are mainly devoted mothers: "Her child shall drag her on the day of resurrection by his navel-cord into the Garden." Their fulfillment, in contrast to males', is seldom described beyond assurances that they will be with their children and husbands, to whom they will still be submissive. The really imaginative picture of women's place in heaven therefore derives from vivid descriptions of saved males' pleasures with the *hur*. For, in addition to the garden's cool breezes, palm trees, flowing streams, and abundant food and drink, there will be dark-eyed, buxom virgins, with flesh so transparent that it reveals the marrow of their bones. In addition to his earthly wives, each man will have seventy such hur, who are not only beautiful, but never sick, menstruating, pregnant (but if he wishes, she will have his child in an hour), bad-tempered, or jealous. Since his heavenly virility will be one hundred times that which he had on earth, he will be able to deflower one thousand hur each month, and find each a resewn virgin when he returns to her. There is a little fear rusting this male projection of the last things, however, because eschatological accounts of Judgment speak of earthquakes, floods, husbands obeying wives, men working for women, and women outnumbering men fifty to one, "resulting in a great increase in ignorance." Masculine desire for women as objects of pleasure therefore runs against a gnawing fear that something in it is unjust and calls for overturning. The result, of course, is another great ambivalence in the image that women bore.

Back on earth and in history, Muslim women were sculpted as much by male honor as by male desire. A woman could not work, for instance, because a husband's honor would be injured, and people would think him incapable of supporting her. In the same way, women frequently were the centers of stormy vendettas caused by insane male jealousy. For the sake of honor, or ego in the bedchamber, women were expected to excel at giving pleasure, yet exhibit great submissiveness and gratitude. On the other hand, honor also caused men to hide their genitals from other men's eyes, forbid the mere mention of another man's wife, and kill a sister at any hint of her marital infidelity. (If her husband killed her he would likely start a blood-feud.) Honor is behind the imagination displayed in popular stories like *Thousand and One Nights,* and the harem system with its endless intrigues. However, because both purdah and polygamy reduced men's access to honorable women, there was a great bottling of sexual feelings in many Muslim cultures. One result of this was an artificial male homosexuality, strongly disapproved by religious leaders, but rife among the wealthy, that degraded many boys and young men. Society put such stress on virility and progeny that genuine homosexuality had no tolerance. The species that spawned, then, was a strange extension of the need to conquer.

In Indian Islam, one finds further nuances to the story of honor, purdah, harem, and polygamy. During the Indian middle ages, harem life lowered the traditional Hindu respect for marriage and motherhood. Because of purdah, Islamic rule also changed the sexes' relations in much of India, for good women no longer could speak to men in public. They had to be veiled, and their lives became circumscribed as never before. A rather rigid distinction developed between good women and lewd, and good women were brought up with the expectation that their marital situation might well be polygamous. Divorce was socially disapproved, so the nubile had to set their caps for compliance and wiliness. Courtesans, on the other hand, needed to be stimulating conversationalists and readily available, so they received a better education and had much more physical freedom. Indeed, *they* were the women romanticized by Islamic India's poetry.

Yet, scholars note, courtesans, and then all women, came to be regarded as temptations or snares. Thus, cautionary tales pictured women accosting travelers, even holy men, with lewd overtures. The image they drew showed men almost helplessly without self-control, so that only the strictest avoidance of women could keep religion pure. Books of piety went on at great length about the dangers in seeing or touching the hands, arms, or face of even a female relative, and each tale, picture, or book added another tile to the mosaic rationalizing purdah. By the fourteenth century, an amalgam of Hindu and Muslim (Sufi) devotionalism produced a fearful interest in yoga and magic, which in turn made for witchhunts and wild tales of females' black powers. Women who were suspected of witchcraft (again usually social marginals) often were forced to undergo trial by ordeal, being burned to death if found guilty.

In Persia, one finds yet another variation on this theme of Muslim women's subjugation. There authorities advised against teaching women to read or write ("a great calamity"), adding, "It were best for a girl not to come into existence, but being born she had better be married or buried." One hadith popular in Persia quoted the Prophet as saying that the essence of the problem with woman is that she stems from a crooked bone (Adam's rib): "If you wish to straighten it you will break it; if you let it alone it will always be crooked." In other parts of the Muslim world, women's crookedness became more graphic. The sexual parts were labeled "the troublemaker," with clear instructions for how to handle them. As late as 1962, clitoridectomy was practiced by Sudanese Muslims, with the rationale that it "releases them from their bondage to sex and enables them to fulfill their real destiny as mother." As well, clitoridectomy is a bulwark against infidelity: "The clitoris is the basis for female masturbation; such masturbation is common in a hot climate; the spiritual basis of masturbation is fantasy; in fantasy a woman broods on sexual images; such brooding inevitably leads a woman to spiritual infidelity, since she commits adultery in her heart, and this is the first step to physical infidelity, which is the breaker of homes" (Bullough, p 143).

Only male prudence and purdah, then, might offset female lust, greed, and weakness in judgment. No wonder that Muslim "sages" developed catalogues of the different female character types (the backbiter, the toadstool), so that grooms might marry the least virulent species of wanton femininity.

It is quite remarkable then, that some Muslim women triumphed over all this misogynism and won fame for purity or learning. Shuhda bint Al-Ibari (d. 1178), for instance, came to be called "the glory of womankind," and her religious learning won her many students. Zaynab bint al-Sha'ri (d. 1219) was another famous woman scholar, while Karima bint Ahmad (d. 1066) is noted as an important transmitter of hadith. Moreover, alongside these intellectuals, whom general circumstances always ensured would be few, there were considerably more female saints. The devotional branch of Islam, called Sufism, was more open to women than conservative orthodoxy, and various orders' rosters of saints included significant numbers of women. Indeed, there were shrines in Cairo, Algeria, and Punjab that were erected in honor of female saints, while today there are thousands of women enrolled in the mystic congregations popular in both North Africa and Turkey.

By far the most renowned female Muslim is Rabi'a al-Adawiyah (712–801), whose biography is mostly legend, but whose cult is quite impressive. At Rabi'a's birth, her father was consoled, since she was the fourth daughter, by a vision that she would be a great saint. Orphaned, sold into slavery, starved, and threatened by evil men, Rabi'a yet survived, due to divine protection. She grew so close to God that human marriage was out of the question, and disciples flocked to her by the hundreds, drawn by her miracles and singlemindedness. Quite different was the life and influence of Walladah bint al-Mustakfi (about 1001–1080), a free-spirited poet from Cordova, Spain. She was the beautiful and brilliant daughter of a wealthy caliph, who defied going customs—she would not marry or be veiled. Her house became a salon for artists and poets, both men and women, and she took three lovers, two men and one woman. Little of her poetry has survived, but her smoking life-style has ensured her immortality.

In traditional Islam, however, the spirited or influential woman was rare. Those who did revolt against their oppression could claim kinship with A'ishah, Muhammad's favorite wife, who when falsely accused of adultery and then vindicated, rebuked both the Prophet and her parents for having doubted her. But little in the established interpretation of the Qur'an or Muslim cultures supported this line of feminist independence. Since the traditional views have only started to crack since the turn of this century, and still are far from fallen, most Muslim women have been treated as semihumans. There are winds of change swirling now, however, so let us turn to the concerns of recent Islamic women.

From the beginning of the twentieth century, largely under the impact of contact with the West, books, poetry, articles in newspapers and magazines began to spotlight the women's issue in Islam. The pioneers in this effort, arousing the ire of traditionalists and vested interests, regularly lost their jobs or had to flee for their lives. The Turkish feminist Halide Edib Adiwar, for instance, barely escaped official prosecution. Polygamy, divorce laws, and purdah were the critics' main targets, and their goal was raising half the Muslim world from a fear, suffering, and ignorance that could only be called slavery. One critique written in 1915, for example, reported on old women who had literally never left the houses they had entered as teen-age brides. When the founder of the Egyptian women's movement, Hada Sh'arawi, publicly removed her veil in 1923, her wealthy husband, who was also her cousin, promptly divorced her. Through the 1930s, the veil became the great shibboleth, progress being measured by feminists according to the degree that women could face the world. By the 1950s, investigative reporters had published the vast extent to which child marriage of girls was practiced and the related soaring incidence of suicide among teen-age women.

Amazingly enough, one can find articles from the 1960s that amount to a traditionalist counterattack: the frequency of Muslim divorce and remarriage, for instance, is a sign of virility. Even in the late 1970s, there are young men defending the veil. They claim that without it they would go beserk and ravage all women in sight. In the same way, they defend polygamy as consistent with nature and their great needs. Even clitoridectomy continues to have its defenders, some seeing it as a way to save women from sin, and others saying that since women's sexual capacity is twenty times that of men, it is necessary if men are to keep dominance and control.

Nonetheless, change is pushing these traditionalists out of the mainstream, due largely to industrialization and its concomitant urbanization, exposure of women to mass media, and revelation of how women live in the non-Muslim world. With greater educational opportunities, because developing Muslim countries need all their peoples' talents, and because they are sensitive to Western criticism, women are being defined less exclusively as domestics and mothers. There has been some progress in both birth control and limiting child marriage, though by no means complete success, and those women who have gained degrees have started to change the complexion of the work force. Affluent women now may be teachers, doctors, or lawyers, for instance, though there is still a strong tendency for them to be specialists in women's education, pediatrics, or family law—which, of course, are the low-prestige areas of their professions.

Middle-class and poor women have faired less well, however, for clerical jobs, factory jobs, and even much domestic work is considered by many as involving too much contact with men and therefore being dishonorable. On the other hand, more middle-class women who develop skills are departing their countries to work abroad, and at home fewer men are willing to assume complete financial responsibility for the women in their lives. Divorcees, for instance, increasingly are expected to find a job. In the countries that have sponsored birth control programs, one finds a higher abortion rate, as well as a higher rate of wife-initiated divorce—signs that women are following through on the control of their lives that birth control can initiate.

To date, however, there is little in the Muslim world that could qualify as a woman's movement. The wealthy and well educated have shown little inclination to lead a charge, probably because it could threaten their privileged status, and the masses are still too mired in poverty and ignorance. The main determinants of liberalization are therefore population control (Muslim women are the most fertile in the world) and pockets of enlightened legislation. Such legislation is cleaning up the disgraces of child marriage, abusive divorce practices, and inheritance inequities, though its implementation and administration are far from excellent. Often religious authorities oppose progressive legislation, and many women are completely ignorant of their new rights. Additionally, in almost all cases —work, voting, education, contraception, travel—it is very difficult for a woman to take advantage of her new opportunities without her husband's or father's approval, for the custom of male dominance dies even harder than specific misogynistic abuses. Difficult to reform, then, is the pressure against wives' initiating divorce, or the pressures for child marriages (the laws are not hard to circumvent). Male honor continues to mean displaying the bride's nightgown to prove her virginity, and men who beat their wives because of jealousy continue to receive suspended sentences from sympathetic courts.

An interesting epitome of this tangle of progress and resistance is modern Algeria. During the one hundred thirty years of French control, both men and women had minimal rights. In fact, French disdain of Muslim traditions caused both sexes to cling tenaciously to purdah, veiling, and polygamy as ways of asserting their Algerian pride. During the war against the French, women joined men as partners—smuggling, spying, bombing, and even taking to Western dress for greater mobility. After peace in 1962, the new constitution provided for sexual equality. Nonetheless, without the pressures of war, the old patterns reemerged, and women were pushed back to subordinate status. For example, the penalty for adultery is twice as severe for women as for men; only men may marry foreigners; the male right to divorce by simple repudiation has been reaffirmed. In the new Algeria, propaganda shouts, it would be unpatriotic for women to divert energies from progress by agitating for social, legal, or economic equality. They should be supportive, stay at home, and distinguish themselves by volunteer charity work.

Under Muslim patriarchalism, women have suffered an oppression that certainly is a strong contender for the title of "world religion's worst." Even here, however, native wit has forged enclaves of self-protection, pride, and creativity. Berber women, for instance, developed a storehouse of liberation songs, telling of grand one-night flings, stinging rebukes to abusive husbands, and other real or imagined delights of freedom. Relatedly, their songs mock the grossness of male's interest in them and debunk men's interest in their motherhood, "to bear boys, boys, and more boys!" In the same way, Tunisian women defy the injustices in their lives and refuse to think themselves second-rate, singing lullabies to their little daughters with lines such as "a girl child is better than ten thousand boys," or "she is my good fortune."

Another line of self-defense has been more explicitly religious: *sar* possession. In Egypt, the Sudan, Ethiopia, Arabia, and Somalia, the common Muslim belief in demons has made possession and exorcism important phenomena, as women regularly become "possessed" in order to gain leverage against their husbands' nearly total power and caprice. In such cases there develops a complex of demands from the possessing spirit (for example, for new clothes or perfume), in strange languages necessitating interpretation (which other women offer for a fee), culminating in parties for the victim and her friends. If the spirit is not exorcised by such obedience, it will render the woman unruly, violent, or sickly—none of which is she responsible for. Many husbands feel that they are being manipulated, but most go along, for they fear that the possession just might be real or escalate if the spirit is not placated. In this way, women have fashioned their own safety valves for the pressures that build up from daily abuse and restriction.

Finally, observers of modern Islamic women's customs note the important role played by the sanctuaries the devotional sects have developed. These are usually humble, but occasionally pretentious, constructions thought to house the presence of a local saint (often they are the saint's tomb, earthly home, or miracle-site). Interestingly, Muslim saints, male and female alike, tended to be socially deviant, and often their deviance included a disregard for the customary relations between men and women, in favor of spontaneity and equality. One saint, for instance, is famous for having renounced his conjugal rights because they interfered with his wife's peace. The sanctuaries function therapeutically for women, because they can find there, in their praying for help, an outlet for their fears (for example, of sterility), angers (for instance, at being beaten), hopes, and so on. In contrast to a doctor, the saint seems nonthreatening, "one of us " (most of the saints were peasants themselves), and inexpensive, for women will make an offering only if their prayers are heard, and they receive the child, cure, or whatever they prayed for.

Furthermore, other women at a sanctuary usually reinforce a sense of having recourse to holy powers, and often the mere outpouring of one's troubles brings some relief. At other times, the onlooker women will gather round and help the petitioner pour out her story, then offer her support, advice, and even concrete material aid. If we remember that women are excluded from the mosque and orthodox religious ritual, we can see that a great deal of genuine faith can be activated through this psychodrama. For it is indeed genuine faith to give voice to one's sense of injustice or seek a way through the boundary problems of evil and death. A limit of the sanctuary system, however, is that it seldom moves out into the marketplace to provoke social change (many local officials support sanctuaries precisely to defend the status quo), yet no one interested in women's real pains could condemn it completely for that. High on the agenda for Islam's entry into the modern world, though, must be the sort of conversions that make sanctuaries less necessary, and women less desperate and more politically powerful.

BIBLIOGRAPHY

Ali, A. Yusuf. *The Holy Qur'an*. New York: Hafner, 1946.

Allgrove, George. *Love in the East*. London: Gibbs & Phillips, 1962.

Bullough, Vern L. *The Subordinate Sex*. Baltimore: Penguin Books, 1974.

Esposito, John L. "The Changing Role of Muslim Women," *Islam and the Modern Age* (February 1976), pp. 29-56.

———. "Women's Rights in Islam," *Islamic Studies* (June 1975), pp. 99-114.

Fernea, Elizabeth Warnock, and Bezirgan, Basima Qattan, eds. *Middle Eastern Muslim Women Speak*. Austin: University of Texas Press, 1977.

Graziani, Joseph. "The Status of Women in the Contemporary Muslim Arab Family," *Middle East Review* (Winter 1976-77), pp. 41-51.

Hodgson, Marshall G. S. *The Venture of Islam, II: The Expansion of Islam in the Middle Periods.* University of Chicago Press, 1974.

Iskander, Kai Ka'us. *A Mirror for Princes.* London: Cresset, 1957.

Levy, Rueben. *The Social Structure of Islam.* Cambridge University Press, 1965.

Lewis, I. M. *Ecstatic Religion.* Baltimore: Penguin Books, 1971.

Mernissi, Fatima. "Women, Saints, and Sanctuaries," *Signs* (Autumn 1977), pp. 101-12.

Mujeeb, M. *The Indian Muslims.* Montreal: McGill University Press, 1967.

Smith, Jane I., and Hadaad, Yvonne. "Women in the Afterlife: The Islamic View as Seen from Qur'an and Tradition," *Journal of the American Academy of Religion* (March 1975), pp. 39-50.

Stiehm, Judith. "Algerian Women: Honor, Survival, and Islamic Socialism," *Women in the World: A Comparative Study,* Iglitzin, Lynne B., and Ross, Ruth, eds. Santa Barbara: Clio Books, 1976, pp. 229-41.

Youssef, Nadia H. "Women in the Muslim World," *(supra)* Iglitzin and Ross, pp. 203-17.

THEOLOGICAL REFLECTIONS

Before reflecting on the theological implications of women's experience with the religions, let us briefly review our data. Recall, first, that at the origins of many cultures women were coequal possessors of humanity, and divinity was androgynous. These two characteristics of archaic societies intersect, but if we begin with humanity we note that women were coequal with men because they had indispensible economic, cultural, and religious roles. Economically, for instance, it was because women beat the bush that men were able to hunt; because women gathered fruits and nuts, men were able to mend their nets and carve their bows. Agriculture, in fact, was quite likely a female discovery and early specialty, for archaic peoples linked it closely with maternal fertility.

Culturally, women's nursing and child-care made them many tribes' repositories of medicinal and poetic lore. Through midwifery, cooking, and gathering they became physicians and pharmacists. Through lullabies and stories they opened children's minds to the past and the way things were thought to be in their world. Religiously, these activities were all sacred, of course, for they all dealt with life's Mystery and power, but women were sacred in their being as well as their doing, since there flowed through them the blood of life. Not surprisingly, therefore, women had a rich cycle of ceremonies designed to inculcate and display their sacrality. The result was that being a woman was a good way to be human.

Because of this, archaic theology regularly was androgynous. That is, in what we condescendingly call primitive cultures, and at the origins of the world religions, the divine Mystery almost always was a female-male wholeness. This testifies to the ultimacy of woman-power, and anyone who has discussed the Great Goddess with women's studies classes knows how such ultimacy continues to work—how hungry contemporary women are for a renewal of their rightful share in God's symbolization. Merely the suggestion that Ultimate Reality is maternal, feminine, "like me," is for many a species of liberation, because it removes a deep source of inferiority.

"In the beginning," then, things were much better, and the fact that the beginning is a matter of myth as much as history only intensifies this judgment. Women know, in other words, that their subordinate status through most of history is a fall from what "must" have been when humanity was new-made. If archaeology or prehistory suggests that this "must" had a religious and social actuality, that there was indeed a time when God was a woman and women wore crowns, it sets fire to a tinder long prepared in oppressed female souls. That is why so many women find archaic religious studies exciting.

Of course, there is danger of romanticizing how things were at humanity's beginnings, and feminist scholars rightly warn us against picturing some matriarchal Camelot. Nonetheless, the foundational insights of even the historic religions confirm how things must have been, for they show that coequal humanity, if not androgynous divinity, was part of the axial seers' vision. For instance, both the Buddha and Jesus associated intimately with women, in contrast to the customs of their times. Muhammad reformed his culture by upgrading the status of women, and the Hebrew Bible taught that humanity was created male and female. Similarly, both members of the Japanese protocouple were equally necessary for the race's beginning; Vedic evidences suggest that ancient Indian women studied and offered sacrifice; ancient China established yin and yang as universal coordinates and set rule in the hands of a royal couple.

Yet, in each of these cases there was a "fall" from the early vision of coequal humanity, and women became subordinate. Hetero-sexuality, in other words, prevailed over common human nature, because men thought women's difference from themselves more significant than their likeness. Unfortunately, the religions connived in this sexism: female Christians were told to be silent in church; female Jews were not called up to read Torah; female Muslims were not welcome in the mosque. In the East, female Hindus could expect moksha only when they were reborn as males; female Buddhists could not become a buddha; and female Chinese were to men as commoners were to kings. Thus, even when the "club" was religion or the "place" was worship, there were signs saying "no women allowed." As a consequence, women the world over received little formal education, were made instruments of males' religious progress, were held to be weaker vessels, and were allied more with nature than with culture.

Worse, most of the major religions came to associate femaleness with the dark, left-handed, irrational, unclean side of reality. Menstruation and childbirth, for instance, regularly were seen as defilements. For that reason, Jewish women had to visit the mikvah each month, Christian women were "churched" (ceremonially fitted back into the community after childbirth), Chinese mothers feared punishment after death as polluters. Islamic, Christian, Jewish, Hindu, and Buddhist sages all considered women more wanton than men—from crooked ribs to daughters of Mara. At its worst, this male projection grounded such practices as clitoridectomy, footbinding, and purdah, which were developed to curb females' deviance.

By today's standards, the religions' histories make them sizable oppressors of women—traditions with a great deal of retribution to make. Few of them have even begun this task, however, and none of them treats women as men's equals. It is only by a selective focusing on the religions' best intuitions, therefore, that one can compose a positive theology or hint at religion's irreplaceable resources. So, having seen the perverse side of the religions, let us conclude by emphasizing the pearls of great price. For convenience and comprehensiveness, we can organize them under headings of nature, society, self, and divinity.

As suggested by archaic religions, women manifest nature's fertility—the awesome power of life—in a special way. Is it possible for us, today, to move beyond the mythology in which this power has been cast and find it a source of pride? I believe it is, though on the way we have to skirt such dragons as "anatomy is destiny." For, despite all such dragons, fertility is a wonder, nature is periodic, and Tao still is beguiling. Fertility is a wonder, because even in a sex-obsessed time, the fruits of love, its squalls and smiles, quicken our pulses, tell us what we are made for. Though populations explode, making birth control imperative, each maternity still invites us to reverence the marvelous scheme of things in which we are placed, the great saga of a life force that has carried us billions of years. Today we have to manage life, yet nature is so vast that we remain more deeply managed. The more we learn of ecology—life's web—the more cautious we become of intervening, and the more our chemical arrogance haunts us with lethal boomerangs. If we are to survive as a species, we shall have to learn to follow nature, rather than ravage it. The religious association of nature with femininity could prove invaluable in this regard.

First, following nature could mean a technology that conceived itself not as exploitation, but as nurture. Our land and our children—how are they best grown? Is there not a central place for gentleness and persuasion? Do we not find that the martial, phallic mind mainly scatters corpses and tears the soil? The sort of wisdom that might nurture life is not that of brahmans or warriors, but that of Prajnaparamita—that which has gone beyond dualism, which moves as music and play. It is a tao, a motherly love. It is a creativity that stays open, turns with the moon, treasures the uncarved block. To today's sensitivities, it is the core of an ecological life-style and thoroughly feminine. So let women rejoice: earth might still be fair, all our children might still be wise, if we love our closeness to life.

This is highflown, but one has only to read a little on world hunger to make it dramatically concrete. Item: Women produce most of the world's food, especially in tropical lands, yet they are virtually ignored when experts from developed countries come to mechanize production and administer the Green Revolution. The result in a country such as India has been that Western aid has benefited only the wealthy and land-rich. The rural poor, fifty percent of whom make less than $5.00 a month, have actually lost ground, largely because no provision has been made for building on Indian women's ties with the land.

Item: Programs for birth control have minimized women's economic roles, though it is clear from China that best success in reducing the birth rate comes when people feel economically secure and no longer need a half-dozen children to provide for their old age. In relation to this, despite much evidence that male contraceptives would be easier to employ and less dangerous than female, women have been chemistry's guinea pigs, resulting in everything from strokes to high abortion rates. Practically speaking, therefore, it may be that only a thorough feminization of the sciences of food production and medicine will make these vital areas truly ecological. A naturalist such as Annie Dillard shows how even nonfarmers and nonphysicians can make such an ecology religious.

SOCIETY

As the history of religions reveals, women have normally been social marginals, ranked with the poor and powerless. Regularly, they have had station, not among the learned and revered, but among the "simple faithful." In Western theological perspective, rooted in biblical notions of justice, this means that women have been, and continue to be, prime candidates for liberation, prime citizenry of the kingdom of God. Let us meditate in this biblical mood for a moment.

Among today's Latin American theologians, who are perhaps the most eloquent and influential expositors of biblical liberation themes, Marxist class analysis combines with the prophetic concerns of the Hebrew Bible and the historical Jesus to forge a powerful credo that God's will is for human beings to do justice, God's way is a suffering love radically opposed to secular power.

In fact, God is said decisively to take sides—to be for the marginalized, against the rich and powerful. It is love that moves the liberationists' God, whether "She" be for or against, but a love as concrete and political as Jeremiah's clash with Jehoiakim, Jesus' clash with the scribes and Pharisees. Only by *praxis*—faith's doing—will one learn what covenant, old or new, really means. Only by uniting love of God with service for neighbor will one keep the divine commandments. Finally, only by realizing that oppression is a social cancer, and that most wealth is sinfully gained, will one have any notion of how radical an overturning a messianic age entails.

These, I take it, are common theses in liberationist theologizing, and one can see their ready application to women's social plight. It is unfortunate that little Latin American theology is sensitive to women's oppression (and it is defaming that black liberation theologians sometimes call the women's movement a racist diversion). Happily, however, women liberation theologians seem determined to keep perspective: subjugated persons ought to fight together, not against one another. For women, equal opportunity is practically nonexistent, no matter what the country or culture. Systematically, sex has joined with money and race to make women akin to the poor and racially despised. This is a fact, even when some of the poor and racially despised are themselves sexist. The biblical assurance that there will be a different heaven and earth, and that they who do prophetic work will reap prophetic rewards (for example, stoning), take women theologians to the depths of what their futures can hold—what they may hope, what love is sure to demand that they suffer. It is no promise of a rose garden, this biblical prophecy, but for many women, as for many Latins and Blacks, it is light and life.

Biblical prophecy, of course, allows only weapons of light, and this underscores a subtler aspect of women's social history. Because they have been officially powerless, women have felt forced to fight with tools of indirection, flattery, manipulation, and guile. Not for them the forthright ways of confrontation, for there lay only derision and defeat. It is remarkable, then, that so many women have preserved a fine sense of concrete justice, embedded in their sensitivity to people and pain. A further result of biblical liberation is that it helps to set this sensitivity free and discourage recourse to guile. By placing one before the radical issues, and inculcating faith that God is allied, if not identical, with our drives for justice and love, biblical religion reworks the rules of the game, reminding us, for instance, how positively and socially Jesus spoke when he asked, "What doth it profit to gain the whole world and suffer the loss of one's soul?"

These are Western terms, but I find their close approximation in Taoist wu-wei. Indeed, as a political tactic, wu-wei is perhaps even more practical than biblical prophecy, for it was forged by people who had no apocalyptic or eschatological expectations—whose horizon was thoroughly this-worldly. Wu-wei, you recall, means "not-doing." It evokes persuasion rather than force, dealing with the difficult while it is easy, valuing inner space as much as outer housing. Why? Because this is how Tao, sacral nature itself, proceeds. For Taoism, as for much feminism, how we proceed—our *process*—is at least as important as our goals, for unless we are human in transit, we will not be human when we reach our goal. If politics is essentially proceeding toward decent life together, we have a lot to learn from wu-wei. The indecencies of our present American life together, for instance, are closely tied to the aggression, force, violence, and ego of our political processes. Because Taoism reacted against a Chinese patriarchalism that had much in common with both biblical and capitalist culture, it is a fine corrective to the phallicism and machismo that threaten even latter-day liberationists. Like Elijah's small still voice, or Jesus' nonviolence, it reminds us that truly religious power, even if it legitimately takes up arms, can never be counter-brutality or counter-hate. Ancient as the seas, supple as the winds, wu-wei disarms by luring opponents to the still point, wins by conversion and change of heart.

SELF

The self of the archaic religious traditions participates in nature's sacrality through various rites of passage. From birth, through puberty and marriage, to death, it has a full curriculum of initiations and revelations. Feminist writers on religion, comparing this rich round of ceremonial experience with the lifecycle of contemporary Westerners, have started to call for the creation of modern rites of passage. These could be especially effective for women, because many of women's life crises are dramatically embodied—the first menstruation, pregnancy, and menopause, for instance. Birth, marriage, and death clearly beg for more meaningful ritualization than our society offers most women, but so do such presently unritualized crises as divorce. Many women have found the time of divorce a terrible desert, largely because nothing happened publicly to play out its end-and-beginning. A prime agendum for feminist theology, therefore, is to rework the traditions' ceremonies, bringing them up-to-date and expanding them, so that our selves may pass through time more meaningfully.

As we have implied in discussing society, today the religious self is also called to participate in struggles for justice and liberation. Whether by prophecy, wu–wei, or other means, religious women are called toward Utopia—the "no place" of what ought to be but has not yet been realized. Theirs, in other words, is a vocation to religious vision—to the wisdom of the New Testament beatitudes, the counsels of Buddhist compassion, and so on. It is no accident that Buddhist compassion connects to a doctrine of no-self, or that Jesus' beatitudes correlate with self-sacrificing love. To understand this, however, one must penetrate Buddhist meditation and Christian prayer. If one does, it appears that the religions' deepest aid for modern women's selves lies in their attack on narcissism and egocentricity.

This does not mean that women, especially, do not have to grow, develop, have a sense of pride, and love their selves. As marginals, with poor social images, women often have not loved their selves, not had a strong sense of their identity and worth. A major reason for developing lifecycle ceremonies of beauty and power, in fact, is to help women grow strong, to make them confident that woman-power and "herstory" are wonderful ways to be human. Having secured this, however, it remains necessary to add that the religions' deepest experients and thinkers speak of fulfillment as a process of self-loss—a process of dropping the fetters of ego, in order to "wander" with Chuang Tzu, or to be mystically espoused with Teresa of Avila.

In Western terms, contemplation enacts self-loss by moving one to concentrate on God. Slowly, it reveals that God has always been prior—has always been the Mystery-ever-greater. Like a lover, the contemplatives' God espouses the self, making life increasingly shared. The Mystery, then, is less and less something apart, more and more one's own horizon and center. Kierkegaard saw this and spoke of the self as a relation to the absolute. Eckhart and Al-Hallaj felt it and spoke of being identical with God. Thérèse of Lisieux exemplified it by not blushing to ask God for flowers. To be a theistic contemplative, then, has been to find one's self by losing it in God, to become whole by loving God with one's whole mind, heart, soul, and strength. In this way, despite their oppression and abuse, the religions have been signal paths to life's depth and goodness. We are all finally overwhelmed by the galaxies, death, stupidity, and our ravaging need for love. Because they alone have a final "amen," the religions alone can "save"—can enable small, overwhelmed selves to hope for eternal meaning.

However, that the religions can free us from personal dead ends and promote self-transcendence does not, for many, prove that religious contemplation is compatible with radical social change. Indisputably, religious contemplation often has not been compatible. Indisputably, otherworldliness regularly has verified Marx's judgment that religion is an opiate, Feuerbach's judgment that God is a vampire sucking out humanity's blood. Still, there are instructive contradictors: Elisabeth Kübler-Ross, who is revolutionizing the care of the dying: Mother Teresa, who is spotlighting the starving of Calcutta; Barbara Ward, who has argued eloquently against an economics that divides the world into rich nations and poor nations. Each has a passion for significant, highly liberating work that she nourishes through explicit openness to divine Mystery.

Three women do not a case make, of course, but they do lay waste the facile assumption that contemplation means apoliticism. More generally, analysis of what is implied in the self's honesty and love, which are the core of contemplation, reveals an intersection of humanistic (as opposed to ideological) feminism and genuine (as opposed to folk or institutional) religion. For genuine religion, whose rarity oppresses the religion-scholar every day, wants just those things that humanistic feminism wants: justice, compassion, freedom. It labors for a society that honors intelligence and goodness; it opposes the privilege, the self-serving—yes, even the sin of those who treat other persons as less valuable than themselves. These, it believes, are the real commandments from God.

DIVINITY

Because the genuine core of the major religions—the vision and love of their founders and saints—beautifies nature, liberates society, and heals the self, it takes human beings toward perfection or "divinity." Divinity is the Mystery both fearsome and alluring, the ultimate reality most real and pure. For all the Western religions, it is the world's beyond and beginning. For all the Eastern religions, it is beauty and truth unveiled. Perhaps the first benefit of religious studies, therefore, is that they concretize our invitation to follow our most human drives and glimpse that for which we have been made. In the silence of the mountains, the humble goodness of people working together, the joy of creativity, divinity touches our lives. It does not matter, finally, whether we recognize divinity as such, nor how we name it. It only matters that we respond to its touch, that we heed its call. We would not seek God, or Atman, or Buddha-nature, or even a just social order, had we not already glimpsed them—were we not already lured by their hope. The kingdom of God, in fact, is but a great symbol for what life would be like if truth and love prevailed. Similarly, moksha, nirvana, and "the Garden" rise from the soul as metaphors for being, awareness, and bliss—for perfection and fulfillment. Religion is therefore as unavoidable and paradoxical as our strange human nature. We can no more deny our intuitions of heaven than we can escape the realities of earth. Religion is a spark from the friction of these two inalienable poles.

Another way of expressing this thought is that the religions keep us aware of the limit-questions in human life—the mysteries of the future, the fullnesses that our hearts dimly sense. In this way, God becomes a judgment on all our idols, for nothing but the holy Mystery may be given total religious allegiance. Thus, there is a great freedom in God, for God relativizes all nonultimacy. Pleasure, wealth, power—these are not the Holy One. Only the term of honesty and love is absolute. The rest is dispensable—as good or as bad as what it does to people's bodies and souls.

One sees, then, that "God" never can be grasped adequately, always is "more" and "beyond." "I am as I shall be with you," Moses heard; you will know me by living in faith, by hoping, by loving. I am not the secure possession of any nation or religious group. Still, Moses and other prophets had to stutter about divinity, so they drew on their cultures' speech. In too many cases, their resultant theology canonized patriarchal biases and limitations (as we have seen only too well). If it remains necessary to speak of God and ultimate reality today (and it does), we must ensure that our language be as undistorting as watchfulness can make it. For women, this means insisting that God is as much female as male (though "She" transcends both), and that ultimate goals have to incorporate the needs, experiences, and depths of women's experiences as much as men's.

So, for instance, if we want to use archaic symbolizations of divine power, we must employ Mother Earth as centrally as Father Sky. If we want to draw on Eastern intuitions of a divine bliss beyond all ego and agitation, we have to think of Prajnaparamita and motherly Tao. When we take comfort from the Islamic and biblical images of divine judgment, of a God who wipes every tear, we must recall how bitterly millions of women have wept. When we invoke Jesus as a paradigm of the care, poetry, suffering, healing, and resurrection to which enfleshing divinity leads, we must stress that women have been powered by his Spirit at least as much as men. Indeed, to redress the imbalance from so many patriarchal times past, we must insist that feminist God-talk and feminist precedence in access to institutional power become high priorities for new popes, head rabbis, Dalai Lamas, or presidents who preach—under penalty of calling their authority incredible.

Finally, because there is a power in feminist religion that I do not find elsewhere, I am sanguine about the future and convinced that the religions' past can teach us well. We cannot escape our past; Santayana is right that those who ignore "herstory" are condemned to repeat its mistakes. The task, then, is to winnow our traditions—to separate the wheat and burn the chaff. Approached in the right way, religion offers a wonderful blend of restlessness and peace. Because of its utopian hopes, we have no lasting city in our present injustices. Because its divinity is always far ahead of us, "prevenient" with support and love, "There lives the dearest freshness deep down things." So, Eastern religion finally blesses women with peace: Shanti. So, Western religion finally shows women, and theological reflectors, their recessional: Long live God.

BIBLIOGRAPHY

Barbour, Ian G., ed. *Finite Resources and the Human Future.* Minneapolis: Augsburg Publishing House, 1976.

Berryman, Phillip E. "Latin American Liberation Theology," *Theology in the Americas,* Torres, S., and Eagleson, J., eds. Maryknoll, N.Y.: Orbis Books, 1976, pp. 20-83.

Carmody, Denise Lardner. "Taoist Reflections on Feminism," *Religion in Life* (Summer 1977), pp. 234-44.

Carmody, Denise Lardner, and Carmody, John Tully. *The Wonder of It All: An Introduction to the World Religions.* North Scituate, Mass.: Duxbury Press, forthcoming.

Cobb, John B., Jr., and Griffin, David Ray. *Process Theology: An Introductory Exposition.* Philadelphia: The Westminster Press, 1976.

Collins, Sheila D. *A Different Heaven and Earth.* Valley Forge, Pa.: Judson Press, 1974.

Dillard, Annie. *Pilgrim at Tinker's Creek.* New York: Harper's Magazine Press, 1974.

Miranda, Jose. *Marx and the Bible.* Maryknoll, N.Y.: Orbis Books, 1974.

Neill, Stephen. *Jesus Through Many Eyes.* Philadelphia: Fortress Press, 1976.

Plaskow, Judith. "The Feminist Transformation of Theology," *Beyond Androcentrism,* Gross, Rita M., ed. Missoula: Scholars Press, 1977, pp. 23-33.

Reuther, Rosemary R. *New Woman New Earth.* New York: Seabury Press, 1975.

Russell, Letty M. *Human Liberation in Feminist Perspective—A Theology.* Philadelphia: The Westminster Press, 1974.

Sobrino, Jon. *Christology at the Crossroads.* Maryknoll, N.Y.: Orbis Books, 1978.

Voegelin, Eric. *Order and History, IV: The Ecumenic Age.* Baton Rouge: Louisiana State University Press, 1974.

Washbourn, Penelope. *Becoming Woman.* New York: Harper & Row, 1977.

INDEX

968006